Wulfrunian Footprints in Fife

by

Robbie Kennedy Bennett

Wulfrunian Footprints in Fife, Copyright ©
Robbie Kennedy Bennett 2014
All rights reserved
The moral right of the author has been asserted

Poetic Writing of Robbie Kennedy Bennett
www.rkbpoetry.co.uk

For my parents, brothers, my wife, children,
our grandchildren and family on our Bennet and Kennedy
journey.

ISBN-13: 978-1502863713
ISBN-10: 1502863715

Introduction;

Poetic pages of time in rhyme from someone with a BLACK COUNTRY and SCOTTISH ancestral background. The common decency of the honest working men that I have toiled alongside and my good family values are all I need to help put my thoughts into words.

There came a time in my life when I looked back as well as forward. Because of my parents I have always thought of myself as being half-Scottish. I was schooled and raised in the town I was born in and played football on most of the football pitches in the area. I also trained myself to be marathon fit by running many miles on roads where generations of my family have travelled and passing by factories that they have worked in. I was a very active young lad and the Royal Hospital, now redundant, was often having me as a patient. As kids my friends and I were finding out who we were when cutting our teeth in the streets and on the local playing fields around the Rough Hills. 'I'm English but I'm also half-Scottish' I would proudly say, 'my dad is from Scotland.' In later years not only did I want to know more about my roots, I wished that I could turn back the sporting clock.

My parents had met in Aldershot Military Hospital whilst in the army and settled in my mothers home town of

Wolverhampton. It was here in 1984 that I ran my first marathon. Although proud of my Wulfrunian roots and up bringing, I have always felt that there is more to me.

My dad had died in 1986 aged 59 and we knew very little of his family background. I myself was busy wrapped up at the time with being a young family man. I was also very focussed on football and running. It was late in the 1980's or early 90's whilst working at Yale Material Handling in Wednesfield when I started putting people or places into verse. Character's in life have always interested me therefore I decided to start writing. I also consider it important to explain to the reader and to remind myself years later, why I wrote the poem.

It was my elder brother who first opened the door to the possibility of us knowing more about our Scottish family history. He had taken a couple of photograph's at the gate of a farm in Fife where our dad was born. If you placed two of those photo's side by side they give you an almost panoramic view of the gate and farm land. I wanted to be there and walk on through those gates and see where it all began, or get as far back as I could. We were to do just that a short while later and were allowed to take a closer look at the cottages.

As explained earlier I was a keen sportsman but age, injuries and work had made me become less active. To be quite honest I was feeling disappointed with myself for allowing my own sporting activities to have taken a back seat. Having ran 10 marathons when in my 30's and played football to mid 40's, in my 50's it was depressing to be doing nothing.

The mood came to a head whilst I was waiting at red traffic lights in Chapel Ash, Wolverhampton. I was recalling the times that the marathon runners had ran from the start on the Ring Road and one of those bobbing heads coming through this way was mine. Then in an instant I thought of the Fife Coastal Path and made plans to see how I could fit walking it into my busy schedule. Yes Fife, where Dad was from, I'll walk it for him!

Poetry Titles

We Knew We Had Love

The Penny Will Drop

A Wulfrunian Way

From Gt Britain to Louisiana

Sarah Ann And The September Sky

I Never Knew Him as Grandad

A Tribute to Nan and Grandad

Welcome to Scotland

The Kingdom of Fife

In My Blood

Be in the Wind Dad

The Old Scottish Stone

She's a Kennedy from Kirkcaldy

Scotland

Collessie

"Can I Help You?" She Asked

Sojourn in St Andrews

Kingskettle Cemetery…Oh Isabella

I Should Have Played For Ladybank Violet

Pull Your Ladybank Panther Shirt Over Your Head

Three Hundred Miles away

Quiet Like in North Queensferry

Thomas Joseph Harris

Grab o' Th' Glass

Ian Understands

When I Walked to Leven

A Friendly Fifer Said "Hello"

Did Alexander Kennedy Walk This Way?

The Silver Trail to Crail

Th' Shores o' Fife

They Walked All The Way From Glasgow

St Andrews I'm On My Way

The Bonnie Bonnie Sand of St Andrews Bay

Falkland Was Lovely Oh Aye

Munro O' Broughty Ferry

From This Window Fife I See

You Keep on Singing Scotland

He Was There With Me Last Night

Bella's Lament

Tell Me O' The Tay

Damn Ye Scotland

I Love The Lomonds

Auld Dundee With Hector

In Through The Door Runs a Little One

Here in The Howe

Auchtermuchty Fields

Highland Infantryman

Home From Home Across The Border

The Cupar Highland Games

The Piper Played by Cupar Hearts
I Thought a Wee While
Fifers in Our Family Tree
A Fifer Burns Inside of Me
A Picture View
You Are Too Far Away
A St Andrews Wedding in June
A Painting by Jack Vettriano
Aberdour Greets Me Kindly
Lovely, Littoral Elie
Only a Field in Kincaple
The Morra Was On The Way to Pettycur Bay
Kingdom Come
Fifers Day 1938
Far Away Scottish Fields
Soldier, Kirkcaldy Soldier
The Terrace of the Bell Rock Tavern
Fife My Friend
This Public Bar in Ladybank
Come Stand With Me in Ladybank
Never Cheer Against Scotland
Scotland Didnae Die
It's What You Are
Thinking o' Fife an' Dundee
Run On With St Andrews United
Cannae See Kinkle Braes Today Mr Traill
The Road That Takes Me Home

Fife am I Early or Fifty Years Late?

The Bridge That I Cross O'er in St Michaels

At Tickety Boo's in Dundee

She Came a' Courting With Me

Red Sunrise at St Andrews

The Strath Won The Fife Cup

Guid Mornin' Isabella

Farewell Isabella

Hurting of Leaving Fife

Saying Goodbye to Fife

Inherent Wolverhampton

May Th' Lovely Lassie

Do I Know You?

Fife is a county on the east of Scotland situated between the Firth of Forth and the Firth of Tay. It adjoins to the west Perth, Kinross and Clackmannanshire. It was once a Pictish kingdom known as Fib. The name 'Pict' as called by the Romans were for people painted or tattooed. Signs of the Picts can be found around Fife. Scotland in this time was named Alba. The Fife region, known as a kingdom is passed down from the Pictish era.

Fife has historic royal connections with Dunfermline Abbey, where Robert the Bruce is buried, minus his heart and Falkland Palace a former home of Scottish Kings. James V1, King of Scotland described Fife as a "beggar's mantle fringed with gold", meaning the coast with its fishing ports. There are more notable buildings and castle ruins spread around Fife.

On a rocky form overlooking the North Sea is the ruin of St Andrew's Castle, built and destroyed several times, as it changed hands between Scots and English in the Wars of Scottish Independence. St Andrews is also well known for being the home of golf and its University.

Fife is without a city but has Edinburgh to the south, Perth to the west and Dundee to the north.

"As the waves cover over
the old Scottish stone,
a thought in my mind
a feeling of home."

"For Fife a flame will burn
as long as I live I will learn,
where I was from and who I am
what is the blood
that runs through this man?"

As mentioned in my introduction, my parents had met in Aldershot Military Hospital whilst in the army. Mom enlisted into the ATS in April 1948, trained in Guildford, then stationed in Liphook, Surrey. After there she was stationed abroad and went out on the Troop Ship 'Empress of Australia' to Fayid in Egypt. After being there a short while she was struck by an army lorry when walking with others. She was the most seriously injured and was sent back to England on the hospital ship 'El-Nil'.

According to dads' Soldier's Record and Pay book, his civil occupation was a Driver Mechanic and joined the army at Aldershot in 1949. He was at the hospital for having had a motorcycle accident.

1

My parents married in 1950 at the Registry Office at Wolverhampton Welfare Services Department on Stafford Street. Their first home was in Blandford, Dorset as dad was stationed at Bovington Army Camp, where my elder brother Gareth was born. My younger brother Stuart and myself were both born in Wolverhampton.

I knew very little of dads' family other than he was from Scotland and we had relations in Risby, Suffolk and as far afield as the USA and Canada.

We had a great childhood on the Rough Hills of Wolverhampton and didn't think of searching into our Scottish past as life seemed fine as it was.

Mom and Dad's Wedding

WE KNEW WE HAD LOVE ©

1996

Above everything that we had
We knew we had love from our mom and dad.
Everything that we got
Things we should do and things we should not.
The time to come in
To where have you been?
You're going to school
Or you'll be a fool.
Have you had your wash?

We was still clean

Though we wasn't posh.

We always went to the sea

My mom and my dad, my brothers and me.

We stayed in digs by the docks,

We'd go to the beach

And play on the rocks.

We didn't have loads of dosh

I've told you before we wasn't posh.

We all knew we were glad,

Of the holiday pay our mom and dad had.

'Cause we always went to the sea.

My mom and my dad, my brothers and me.

And above everything that we had

We knew we had love from our mom and dad.

Thanks Mom and Dad for a great childhood

Fortunately we grew up in a family with parents that wanted to get out and enjoy the outside. Dad was a long distance lorry driver so always knew of places to go to. We were always amazed of wherever we were that someone would say "Hello Jock" to dad.

Great Yarmouth was a favourite seaside town of ours and time spent on the sands and down at the docks was memorable. What is vivid is not long after first arriving at the beach, dad would turn up with a blown up lorry tyre for us kids to play in the sea with. We felt special as this was not your ordinary beach toy.

The building of sandcastles was exciting and this is where I can first recall the Scottishness in our family other than our dads accent. The flags that you buy from the seaside shops and the Rampant Lion was always my favourite. Even to this day, 50 years or more later, whenever I see that flag it reminds me of our holidays on the beach at Great Yarmouth.

Both sides of mother's family for three generations before her were mainly from Wolverhampton and the surrounding area. She had a sister and brother-in-law living in Harlow, Essex whose son Piers is as close as a brother to me. We were raised on a new estate built on the east side of town in the 1950's. Although she had had grown up the other side of town she was within a mile of the All Saints area where she was born. Unfortunately Mom was to find that her birth mother died of Pneumonia.

It was later on in life that I wanted to know more of who we were and our own personal family story. I suppose that there are many individuals who can relate to this stage in life as they grow older.

The Penny Will Drop ©

2005

When young you simply don't see it
when middle aged you wish that you had,
the roots of the life you are living
and you may become Mom or Dad.
Some have questions without answers
for those who can help have passed on,
like a show without music and dancers
the show as they say must go on.
Your elders will give information
details that you want to know,
go get the answers for questions
before it is their time to go.
You may be surprised what they tell you
it is not such a difficult task,
your children today have no interest
but the penny will drop and they'll ask.

I wrote 'A Wulfrunian Way' in November 2006 and was delighted to find it being featured on the Black Country Memories page by Dr Carl Chinn in the Express and Star the following month.

Amongst the report he had mentioned 'this indelible bond between yesterday, today and tomorrow is strengthened in A Wulfrunian Way by an intuitive feel for the place that draws out a sense of oneness with Wolverhampton'.

A Wulfrunian Way ©

2006

I descend from a working class background;
I grew up in a town of my mothers' line.
I live everyday a Wulfrunian way,
And there is nothing that I want that is not mine.

There are family names scattered all around,
Roots of mine are in this town,
Within the soil deep in the ground.

Goodyear company my grandad served,
Long service recognition was well deserved
I can always find a family name,
From Bushbury and Graiseley to Steelhouse lane.
Williams, Rowley and Owen have seen,
World wars and coronations of Kings and Queen.

We've walked down St Peters steps to the market,
Shopped at the open stalls.
Waited at the stops for trolley buses,
And sat on the old church walls.

We've seen vehicles drive down Dudley Street
And been struck by the light in the old Arcade.

Many a relation at All Saints was taught,
And many a present from Beatties was bought.

We've stood on the terraces at Molineux,
The great days my relations have seen.
We were here before the racetrack at Dunstall,
Before greyhounds and speedway at Monmore Green.

The Mander Centre came,
And shoppers descending from a family name.
Williams, Rowley and Owen have been,
The town of Wolverhampton changes we've seen.

Prince Albert on his horse wasn't always there,
He's moved a few times since he came to Queens Square.
New buildings in town that's now called a city,
Some perhaps fine and others not so pretty.

Relations have worked at Chubbs,
And been the licensee of pubs and clubs.
The Royal Hospital treated our troubles and woes,
Our cuts and scars and nursed our bloody nose.

It's fair to say, in every way,
We've worked and toiled and earned our pay.
And It's fair to say, that everyday,
We've lived our life a Wulfrunian way.

Crown Coin

Yes, we lived our life a Wulfrunian way and just got on with who we were, a family living in Cheviot Road on the Rough Hills with relations scattered around the town. I grew up knowing of dad's relations and we often received letters that continued to arrive addressed to mom after dad had passed on.

I was to receive a gift a few years ago of a Crown coin from our relation Joan in Louisiana, that had been given to her around 40 years earlier by my dad.

From Gt Britain to Louisiana, Ten Bob Time a Shilling and a Tanner ©

2006

This crown coin transferred from hand to hand,
This crown coin went with her to another land.
It travelled many miles,
And it brought back many smiles.
She received this gift of a coin with pleasure,
Lovingly cherished, her piece of treasure.

In almost two score years,
There's been love and happiness shared with tears.
From Gt Britain to Louisiana,
Ten bob time, a shilling and a tanner.

This crown coin reminded her of another age.
Kindred love, in an early chapter, on another page.

And she never did forget it so,
Back to Gt Britain this coin did go.
She conveyed this coin with kindly words to its motherland,
With kindred thought it's now entrusted in another hand.
He received this gift of a coin with pleasure,
Lovingly cherished, his piece of treasure.

For he knew how much she thought of the one,
Who gave her the coin and he has gone.

This crown coin showing Churchill's face,
In another hand, another place.

In almost two score years,
There's been love and happiness shared with tears.
From Gt Britain to Louisiana,
Ten bob time, a shilling and a tanner.

From Gt Britain to Louisiana by Robbie Kennedy Bennett

As I grew into my middle aged years my feelings were that I had not put enough thought outside of my immediate family. There was so much that I didn't know and although I may have been told many times the reality of it all did not set-in.

I wrote Sarah Ann and The September Sky with careful consideration of the two people I consider of being my Grandparents in Wolverhampton. My brothers and myself loved them wholeheartedly. Sad circumstances concerning our maternal Grandmother but love overcome of which we are thankful. Sarah Ann, died within weeks of our mother's birth.

On another note, on the first day of September 2013, at the time of writing, the sky was a colourful delight. Coincidently it was also noticed by a cousin of mine.

SARAH ANN

AND

THE SEPTEMBER SKY ©

2013

September sky
Striking it is, oh why?
As I try to write of, Sarah Ann

A Sunday light blue
And I'm writing of you
A Sunday light blue, Sarah Ann, I can see
As the evening draws in, gradually

Fifty nine summers so far
Fifty nine summers
None shared with Sarah Ann
My maternal Gran, Sarah Ann

A father of two I became
Feels good to tell you and write your name
Bloodline, from the same
Aren't we Sarah Ann?

Fifty nine summers
Fifty nine summers, Sarah Ann, I have had

Four children call me Grandad
And for your daughter, my mother, I am glad
Sarah Ann, your story is sad

Motherhood, a premature end
Your six children couldn't comprehend
From newborn up to aged eleven
Asking why, their mother, had to go to heaven?

A mother of three boys, your baby daughter became
Feels good to tell you and write your name
Into my mind you came
My maternal Gran, Sarah Ann

We missed you Sarah Ann
In the passing of time
Now, Sarah Ann
You are sharing these minutes of mine

September sky
Amazing, why oh why?
As the sky is red Sarah Ann
And now, a Sunday dark blue

A Sunday dark blue
As I'm writing of you

A Sunday dark blue, Sarah Ann I have said
Is it you in that September sky, that September red?

That September red, Sarah Ann I have said
If true, Sarah Ann, if true
My fifty ninth summer
... Then I've shared this summer with you!

I Never Knew Him as Grandad ©

2005

I never knew him as grandad
I loved him, who stood in his place,
I grew up without understanding
Not thinking to picture his face.

In a time of worries and troubles
An age of conflict and war,
Who is the man in the photo?
To my thoughts I open the door.

His regiment was the 4TH Lincoln's
Held captive but made his escape,
Wounded by a bullet in a shoulder
Desperate and in poor shape.

The battlefield he crawled for four days
Drinking water from bottles of dead,
French Officers saw movement in a body
Injured by bullets of lead.

Discharged in 1918
In his regiment he could no longer be,
He was no longer physically able
A young man of just twenty-three.

He lived on to be forty-one
But pneumonia set in and he died,
I never knew him as grandad
Then inside a part of me cried.

Yes, I wrote Sarah Ann and I Never Knew Him as Grandad as I had a feeling that I should do and doing so has connected us. The very fact that I wrote about them both makes me miss them. Having said that, we were very lucky as these two people were lovely and we were having a happy childhood.

A Tribute to Nan and Grandad ©

1991

My Grandad was a quiet man
But still liked family around.
While Nan sat there talking
He'd hardly say a sound.
Sitting in his armchair
Hearing others talk,
Never ever offending
Often liked to walk.
I can see him in his suit and tie
Looking neat and smart,
My Grandad was a quiet man
With the biggest kindest heart.

My Nan she always told stories
Of the old days and years gone by,
She must have been a young rascal

20

I can tell by that look in her eye.
The cheekiest grin on a lady
Will never be seen no more,
I'm sure up in heaven God's smiling
Since Jane Rowley has passed through his door.

The years passed by too quickly, I fell in love, we got married quite young, parents of a boy and a girl who were both to grow to be wonderful parents themselves. Amongst all that Dad had died in the mid 1980's. When he did so he took with him all we wanted to know later in life of our Scottish family history.

A late friend of mine named Hedley Farr was forever encouraging me to make the effort and go to Scotland. He was a former neighbour of mine and we shared a Sunday evening drink for many years.

It was my elder brother who first found the places in Fife and soon for my wife and I were to go with him. I had always been proud of who we were and where we were from albeit from a distance, now I was finally making the journey.

Gretna, Scotland

Welcome to Scotland ©

Forgather with Fife

2006

I recall the field I played upon
Even though my childhood has passed and long gone
And I also recall my honest upbringing
The school of All Saints and the church choir singing

Inside of my home there spoke a scotch voice
The sound of my father so I had little choice
To grow as I did in a loyalty divide
A part of my make up is Scottish inside

Later in life it had greater effect
I feel quite at home in Scottish dialect
A definition was needed therefore
I searched for my soul outside of my door
Whenever I can in my year I depart
To the land that grew strong in the depth of my heart

The Midlands of England I leave in my wake
A pilgrimage journey I take
Lancashire looms well into my drive
To the land of Caledonia that keeps me alive

At Kendal the scenery catches my eye
The miles that I travel drift on by
Not far from Carlisle I see the sign
Welcome to Scotland
It feels so divine
Never do I hurry through the borderland
The beautiful picturesque borderland

Edinburgh and Glasgow point my way
On the journey I make on that day
To a homeland I repeat in the depth of my heart
I'm sad come the day when I have to depart
Disown I shall never my forebear behind
Caledonia completes and questions my mind

I had finally arrived in Fife and it had been a long time coming, too long to be honest with you. My elder brother Gareth had made that breakthrough as he showed us around Collessie. I was in awe of the peacefulness and impressed by the fact that our dad was born in such a beautiful place. As we were driving past dwellings in Monkstown, Ladybank, my wife Lynne caught sight of a name plaque on a wall. Later back at home and after studying an old photo of dad's, comparing with one that we had taken, a feature upon a wall proved that it was his former home.

From then on the long drive to Fife was a regular occurrence and researching proved to be fruitful up to a point. Names, trades, etcetera were found in many towns and villages, especially on the coast of Fife from Kirkcaldy to St Andrews.

Lomond Hills

THE KINGDOM OF FIFE ©

2002

It's pleasing to be where you've been,

And to see what you've seen,

The fields of farmers corn,

The cottage in where you were born,

Those lanes with walls of stone,

Did you run or wander and roam.

Could you see the smoke from the railway,

Rise over the Kingdom of Fife,

Have you stood on Ladybank station,

Was it happy your childhood life.

The Lomond Hills stand high,

27

As high as the Scottish sky.
Is that where you wanted to be,
Did you want to climb them to see,
North to the Firth of Tay,
The church of Collessie or Cupar,
And out to St. Andrews bay.
Did you ever ride out to the ocean,
Watch the fishing boats mooring at Crail,
Was the sea your only tomorrow,
How soon were you likely to sail.
Your bloodline runs on now in England,
Bennet Kennedy roots lie in Fife,
We honour the land we are living,
But The Kingdoms a part of our life.

To be in the land where ancestors before me took a grip, drawing me there as often as I possibly could. I was soon to get used to the overnight driving and early starts. Words cannot explain the feeling that comes over me when in Fife.

I can recall this one visit being down by the Forth Rail Bridge and looking at the magnificent structure. My Fife ancestors would have seen or heard of the bridge growing over the Forth. It surely would have been the news of the the day.

In My Blood ©

2005

When realising Fife was in my blood,
On that land I proudly stood.
No nae more will we be apart,
It's in my mind and in my heart.
This part of Scottish land is home,
It's in my skin and in my bone.
Wherever I travel, whatever I see,
In my blood Fife will be.

Even to this day I track my mind back to the time when I should have been asking questions. There has been many times when I have thought "if only I …......"

I wrote 'Be In The Wind Dad' in1994 when being aged 40 and married to my wife Lynne for 20 years. Our two children, Marie and Steven were aged 14 and 12 at the time.

I was still dealing with losing my dad 8 years earlier and wanting to keep him in my life. Little did I know that this would be very much so come the new millennium.

Be In The Wind Dad ©

1994

Be in the wind dad
And in the rain,
Be in the hurt dad
Remove all the pain.

Be in my step dad
Wherever I walk,
Be in my words dad
Whenever I talk.

Be in my nights dad
And in my days,
Be in my moves dad
And in my ways.

Be in my strength dad
Don't let me bend,
You were there at the start dad
Be there at the end.

Th' Auld Scottish Staine, as said in Scottish dialect, was written after a stay in St Andrews, Fife, Scotland. I was there for the weekend on football related business at the University sports ground.

This short stay in St Andrews made a great affect on my life. I was staying in digs just around the corner from the famous Old Course and I would stand by the sea as the waves crashed against the rocks. I would go there after breakfast and in the early hours before retiring to my room. On this one occasion a mini bus turned up and a group of American golfers disembarked. They were laughing and joking understandably within their holiday mood. For a moment I had an imposing feeling. I soon collected my thoughts and reassured myself that I had roots all around this part of Scotland and I had a belonging to the Kingdom of Fife.

In time I was to find that I was walking back and forth past the streets and dwellings of where my St Andrean ancestors had their first and last days.

A few weeks had passed by until I actually decided to write the poem. I have the feeling now that I have 'bottled' a special time in my life that resurfaces whenever I read it. The Old Scottish Stone is to be read as if I am in conversation with the sea and land.

THE OLD SCOTTISH STONE ©

2002

What should I be thinking?
Or should I say,
As I stand on the coast
At St Andrews Bay.

The homeland of golf
The American voice,
They come to The Kingdom
They come of their choice.

As the waves cover over
The old Scottish stone,
A thought in my mind
A feeling of home.

For Fife a flame will burn
As long as I live I will learn.
Where I was from and who I am
What is the blood?
That runs through this man.

Like the flags I am flying
Like the stones I am grey,
I've a bold Scottish passion
That won't wash away.

St Andrews a town that's so proud
A voice in the wind that speaks loud,
"The blood in that man is still strong
To remember your roots is not wrong".
The clouds may get heavy
The stones may be grey,
The sea tells St Andrews
"He won't wash away".

'So you tell The Kingdom
And tell all your shores,
It's as much as its mine
As it is yours'.

The Kingdom now answers
"Why don't you learn?
"Why don't you forget us?
"Why does your heart yearn?

'How can I forget you?
I've blood in this land,
Have they stood where I'm standing?
And walked on this sand.
Have they breathed what I'm breathing?
This brisk Scottish air,
Why did they not want him?
Why did they not care?

"They may have loved him
Though he did not know".
'But did someone hurt?
To let that boy go'.

35

'He was born in your land
And he grew strong,
I am his son
And I know I belong.
So you tell your seas
And tell all your shores,
I'll still breathe this air
Even though you shut doors'.

The clouds may get heavy
The stones may be grey,
"You've a bold Scottish passion
That won't wash away".

***

The sun slowly shines over Fife…
It cuts through the clouds like a knife.
It shines on this glorious land
The sea and the beautiful sand.

'So you tell The Kingdom
And tell all your shores,
It's as much as it's mine
As it is yours'.

***

St Andrews Bay now glistens
As the sea hits the land it listens,
Although I stand here all alone...

They won't cover over this old Scottish stone.

I was at a stage in my life of wanting to know more as I had missed the opportunity of asking in my dad's lifetime. Why was the name of Kennedy in the family and why does our Bennett have a double 't' at the end? This was asked of me when speaking to someone connected to our line in Toronto. Dad may not have known the answers himself but at the very least it may have opened up other interesting facts.

What I did find is that our Kennedy link is to Kirkcaldy and along that coastline. More often than not Kirkcaldy was to become the first resting place when arriving in Fife so perhaps I was being drawn here?

I gaze at the Forth knowing that this would be the view that my ancestors would have seen.

She's a Kennedy from Kirkcaldy ©

2006

She worked on a farm in her teenage years
Did she warm to Collessie or cry some tears
Were her clothes so smart or shoddy?
Only her name and not her face
Is all that I had for me to trace
She's a Kennedy from Kirkcaldy.
Yes I only knew her name,
Knowing where she's from but then became
Her blood runs through my body.
And what colour was her eyes and hair?
Deep inside she will be somewhere
She's a Kennedy from Kirkcaldy.

Scotland ©

2006

Scotland you call me once more
Come to the land of your father,
And his mother and father before.
Come over the hills of the borders
They roll for many a mile,
Come where they sing of the heather,
Come and stay for a while.
Scotland in bright summer sunshine
Scotland when raining and wet,
Scotland in winter as snowflakes fall
Your roots you will never forget.
The beauty and charm of Scotland
Is a welcome to one and all,
When the bagpipes play on Hogmanay
Scotland again will call.
Come to the land of your father,
And his mother and father before,
Come to the land of your father,
An' before an' before an' before.

Our Dad was born in 1926 in Collessie, Fife, and grew up not too far away in Ladybank. Collessie is a small hamlet in central Fife about 3 miles east of Auchtermuchty surrounded by steep little lanes and farmland. My dad was born in a cottage on a farm. My elder brother had found this farm on an earlier visit to Fife and took a picture by the gate showing the name.

When he next came it was with my wife and I and we decided to venture further. There was a working area on the farm by a building where I knocked on the door. This man appeared and after listening to why we were here granted us permission to look around the outbuildings where dad was born. From this farm you can clearly see the Lomond Hills to the south west.

Dad, as a wee laddie

It was a special moment in my life to be at dads' birthplace and from the cottage garden I used my mobile phone to call our Mother to tell her where we were.

From there we visited the village of Collessie and found it to be a peaceful charming place. There is a little stream surrounded by homes with pretty tended gardens. The church of Collessie is picturesque and can be seen for many miles. This village is only a short distance from the road to Cupar and on to St Andrews. At the crossroads at the Howe of Fife you can travel northward up to Dundee.

There is no sign now of Collessie Castle that stood west of the kirk or Rossie Loch by the Howe of Fife, which was drained in 1740.

Pilgrims on their way to the shrine of St Andrews would pass through Collessie on route. This church was opened in 1839 and had many predecessors. In the kirkyard wall is an inscription that begins…

Ye laden pilgrims passing on your way,
Think of your fall and your offences past…

This family of pilgrims left the charming hamlet of Collessie and like many more over the centuries travelled to St Andrews.

A few years went by before I wrote my poem titled 'Collessie' and I became a proud man when I received a request for the poem to be on the village website. My lovely little springtime poem was wanted at her home.

Collessie ©

2006

Collessie, I walked your peaceful lanes in springtime,

Time stood still as I walked your lanes in springtime.

Flowers in their beds not long from birth,

Planted with care in God's pure earth.

Collessie, I walked your peaceful lanes in springtime.

I rested a while by the Kirk yard wall,

The square tower and spire, standing tall.

Collessie, I walked your peaceful lanes in springtime.

Thatched cottage buildings made by hand,

And weavers' homes they still stand

The handlooms that once would echo around,

It's different now for I hear no sound.

Collessie, I walked your peaceful lanes in springtime.

Time stood still as I walked your lanes in springtime.

I rested a while by the Kirk yard wall,

The square tower and spire, standing tall.

High in the Kirk is a view to behold,

In weavers' homes, are there stories to be told?

Collessie, I walked your peaceful lanes in springtime.

Quite often when in Fife I like to stroll around the lovely quiet lanes and take in the peacefulness. Sometimes I can be there for a while without seeing anyone. I often wonder if my dad had ever done the same or even if he knew that he was born here?

Collessie has a beautiful church and on this one visit before my road home a lady surprised me by asking a question as I walked the lane. I could not be sure if she thought that I looked suspicious or lost as I was in a daydream. Looking back I should have engaged more into a conversation.

This one morning there was an interesting message in my website Guest Book;

GUEST BOOK MESSAGE
I was born and brought up in the village of Collessie and my parents lived in the house that is shown on your main picture beside the church they lived there for 43 years. I am curious to know why you wrote about the wee village that has really changed beyond recognition for the wee hamlet it was in the 1960/1970's. Regards Alison

ADDITION VIA E-MAIL

Thank you for replying to me and of course you may display my message I am very proud of being a Collessie "bairn" (you had to fall in the burn to be christened that!!). I wonder who farmed Hahill when your father was born I know that it belonged to the Storrar family before the Barrs took over. Alison

"Can I Help You?" She Asked ©

2011

"Can I help you?" she asked,
did I seem suspicious?
I'd come a long, long way
to walk and talk to no one in particular,
whoever wants to walk and talk today?
Delightful was Collessie,

Did I seem suspicious,
did I look lost? perhaps I am,
perhaps I can't, perhaps I can,
find out where I am going to
Collessie, you are beautiful,
Collessie you are you.

"Can I help you?" she asked,
Perhaps she can't, perhaps she can,
perhaps I should have walked,
perhaps I should have ran,
ran to where I'm going to,
Collessie, you are beautiful,
Collessie you are you.

St Andrews is historic and interesting and has kept its identity over the changing of time. With castle ruins, university, cobbled streets and wynds that make you feel you are in a Sir Walter Scott novel or a Robbie Burns poem.

My great grandmother came from here and her family would have walked the very streets that inject my imaginative mind. She was born in the shadow of St Rule's tower and the ruins so ancestral feelings in St Andrews are very strong.

In time I was to find addresses of ancestors, places of births, marriages and deaths, one by one I searched for those former dwellings. This one particular house, which in 1871, I believe was the home of James Traill, my Gt. Gt. Grandfather. This dwelling is the last of the pillared forestair in St Andrews and often seen in photographs.

It appears that we were in the Fisher Quarter, as it was known, with addresses in North St, Abbey St, South Castle St and Bakers Lane. These in time would be part of the route of my early morning walk.

Sojourn in St Andrews ©

2006

Walking along the historical streets of St Andrews,
I love to leisure timelessly.
I stroll on beyond the famous Old Course
And absorb the wash of the sea.
The sound of the ocean is tranquil
And the springtime weather is mild,
I've so much to learn about life and belonging
I feel like a newborn child.

The coastal grey stones
Break the waves by the shore,
I stand and admire
Like my forefathers before.
Did they walk the same streets?
Stand in the same place,
Hear the waves crash,
Feel the wind in their face.

In thought I pass the family divide,
My feelings are stirring deep down inside.
What's in my character?
And inside my blood,
Is there anything of value or misunderstood.

Images appear in my picturesque mind,
They tempt and they tease
Are they being unkind?
Ancestors before with faces unknown,
By this sea and this land
Seeds they have sown.

Strolling back and forth to Shorehead,
The castle for a while mesmerised me.

This ruin contends the test of time,
And still stands proud majestically.

Tis like an old parent with the sense to protect,
Even though their prime has long gone.
The elements surpass this armoury of stone,
And pilgrims still appear to look on.

My ancestors would have seen this too,
The Cathedral and the coastal view.
Ancient steps to an image of a door,
The sea as it blankets the rocky shore.

Along the east coast
I gaze with a naked eye,
Hills far away change shades of their colour
As the sun breaks a cloudy sky.
The Firth of Tay is over the horizon
Too far for me to see,
Blue skies are afar
A sunny day up in Dundee.

A stroll by the coast at St Andrews
Is a walk back in time for me,

Of all of the sands I have trod in my years
This is the shore I should be.

These thoughts as I pass the family divide,
Is there more than St Andrews stirring inside?
Bennet and Kennedy, Cramond and Traill,
With roots all around I shall prevail.

One day will I hold another by hand?
One day if I tell them will they understand?
There's a spiritual call to this coast, this shore,
I'm part of this land, a Bennet and more.

My Great Grandmother and more
Born in St Andrews

We started to make visits to Fife as often as we could and this one day we were directed to Kingskettle Cemetery from someone in Ladybank. We entered the gate to find men working on one side therefore we started our search amongst gravestones on the other side. Within a minute or so of being able to look where the workers had been, Lynne was to call me.

Kingskettle Cemetery
…Oh Isabella ©

2006

Dedicated to the families
Traill and Bennet

In Kingskettle Cemetery I stand
Looking at a stone on a piece of land
I read some names I thought I'd never see
In this place I thought I'd never be

Oh Isabella I read your name
I found from St Andrews on the coast you came
Oh Isabella you didn't know me
But I think about you by the sand and the sea

Whenever I cross the Firth of Forth
From home to home on my journey north,
My heart fills up with inner pride
It beats with the passion that I feel inside.

But there are too many faces I do not know
And there are too many miles I have to go,

To get this close to get this near
To get to the land that I love so dear.

Oh Isabella I read your name
I found from St Andrews on the coast you came
Oh Isabella you didn't know me
But I think about you by the sand and the sea

I read on the stone you were the last that died
So I'm standing where you would have stood beside
You don't know me your great grandson
Standing on the ground you would have grieved upon

Oh Isabella I read your name
I found from St Andrews on the coast you came
Oh Isabella you didn't know me
But I think about you by the sand and the sea

In Kingskettle I leave behind
Names on a stone I thought I'd never find
Oh Isabella you didn't know me
But I think about you by the sand and the sea

In August 2013 there was a message for me from a lady who believes she is Isabella's cousin, maiden name of Reid and living in Canada. Her Grandfather was Pa Reid, the Dentist and she was taught to dance by Isabella in the family home. I have found that surname in research of our family tree, possibly from Dundee.

Planning to walk the Fife Coastal Path as mentioned came when at a set of red traffic lights at Chapel Ash in my home town of Wolverhampton. I was visualizing hundreds of bobbing heads coming running towards me half-a-mile into the Wolverhampton Marathon in the mid eighties, one of those heads was mine. I was working hard at the time and had been having sporting depressing feelings for a while and wished that I had my time all over again.

I should have gone to Scotland to play football or in later years ran a marathon now and then. Why didn't I do something for Scotland when young, fit and more than able. I have a few photos of myself running in a pair of blue Scotland shorts. At the very least I put it into the written word in 2007.

Ladybank

I Should Have Played For
Ladybank Violet ©

2007

Not ever in my sporting prime,

Whatever talent I had of mine,

And skill that I did unearth,

Did I take to the land of my fathers' birth.

I should have played for Ladybank Violet,
A scout may have seen me and signed for Dundee.
I could have been capped for Scotland,
That's what I would have chosen for me.

But I never played for Ladybank Violet,
I've never graced a Fife football field.
I've not scored a goal in the league or a final,
In Fife I've not won a cup or a shield.

If I had one wish I'd go back to the day,
When I could run from the Forth to the Firth of Tay.
What a fantastic idea,
I should have gone for a few weeks in every year.

But it's too late now and no matter how it may seem,
I've done it all, I've done it within my dream.
In that dream I'm representing Scotland,
That's everything I wanted to do.
And if my dad was alive,
I'd tell him I did it for you.

In 2007, the day before what would have been my dad's 81st birthday, I sent the poem and the story to the Fife Amateur Football web site. Within hours Jimmy, the administrator had replied with the following message,

'Thank you so much for a fantastic email'.
'Wishing you all the best and it's never too late to score a goal on a Fife football playing field.'
Jimmy, Fife Football website.

I toasted another milestone returning to my dad's roots by opening a bottle of McEwan's, Scotland's award winning ale, cheers dad.

Dad

I can only assume that dad was educated locally such as Ladybank Primary Primary School. I did make contact with the school but unfortunately they held no records of that time. Upon researching the school I found that it was built around 1860 and no doubt he or others in his family would have attended. In August of 2014 when in Ladybank, I stopped by to take a photograph of the school wondering if this was my father's childhood playground?

Concerning the Ladybank football recognition, I did not know that there was a football interest in the village. This would be my ignorance and soon there was to be other football news coming out of Ladybank.

This one week I noticed a picture of the lads from Ladybank Panthers FC visiting Bayview, home of East Fife FC. There they were in the tunnel and the stand, in the same team and probably sharing the same dream from Ladybank, Fife my dads village.

My poem "Pull Your Ladybank Panther Shirt Over Your Head" reached those deservedly so;

"I was drawn to your site by the poem on Ladyank Panthers. I founded the club a few years back so it was nice to see the recognition you had given it. Thank you".
Michael Fox , 17 April 2010

Those words were rewarding and inspiring.

Pull Your Ladybank Panther Shirt Over Your Head ©

2009

In a picture of Ladybank Panthers,
the laddie's they were a grinning.
Schoolboy dreams, football teams,
losing drawing or winning.

There in the Fifer's ground,
in Bayview they were looking around.
Could you imagine running out on that pitch?
A football career brings cheers and tears,
some can be famous and rich.

But how about playing to enjoy,
everyone of you laddie's a happy wee boy.
One day you may look back on that day,
here's what this footballing poet does say.

Pull your Ladybank Panther shirt over your head,
don't play to be dirty and don't be misled.
Play hard you Panthers play fair,
Bayview, Hampden, anywhere.
Whatever field you Panthers may grace,

keep the Ladybank Panther smile on your face.
Never mind being famous or rich,
be proud to be out on that pitch.

Pull your Ladybank Panther shirt over your head,
don't play to be dirty and don't be misled.
Play for the Panthers play for your name,
play football the greatest game.

In the early spring of 2007 I was feeling the desire of a new challenge while there was still enough life left in me having past my 53rd birthday. My football and marathon running days were well past because of dodgy ageing knees. A medical verdict a few years back described the problem as 'excessive wear and tear'. By now life had moved on from my sporting competitive days and my wife and I were now grandparents for the first time.

All my sporting years had been based in the Midlands and I prided myself on running many of the local marathons in the mid 1980's. The Wolverhampton Marathon was on my calendar a few times as were Sandwell and Birmingham. Many roads around the Black Country were in my training programme and my A–Z at the time was well marked out with mile marks for my reference. The Black Country Bugle has printed many poems of mine over the years portraying my affiliation to the Midlands. A Wulfrunian Way describes in verse my family roots on my mom's side. Carl Chinn also featured this poem in the Express and Star during Christmas 2006 calling it a 'cracking poem Rob'. He was true to his E-mail by printing it with a picture of St Peters church overlooking the old outside market. Carl described it as capturing Wolverhampton how he and his family feel about Birmingham. Kind words from a man who is passionate about local history.

I had recently regretted not going to my dad's birthplace when in my sporting days. This resulted in a poem of mine I Should Have Played For Ladybank Violet. Often when visiting my roots in Fife I had noticed the Coastal Path stretching the 82 miles from the Forth and Tay bridges. I began to believe this could be an opportunity of a suitable challenge and to balance the books of my parental divide. The walk can be done in stages so I started to make plans for at least 2 days.

On the evening of Sunday 13 May at 7.45pm I set out from my home in Codsall for a leisurely night time journey, resting on route to Scotland. The weather through the night was poor until I had got past the Lake District. I eventually arrived in Fife driving over the Forth Road Bridge at 5.00am on Monday morning. The magnificent sight of the Forth Rail Bridge in North Queensferry greeted me not long after dawn.

I parked my car at the railway station at 5.30am and searched for the start of the Fife Coastal Path. My plan was to get to Burntisland, 13 miles along the coast where I had booked 2 evenings bed and breakfast.

To be completely honest I struggled to find the start of the path and at 5.30am in the morning there wasn't anybody in sight to help. When in the middle of a short panic attack the sign of the coastal path was there before me, as if to say, 'here I am, open your eyes'. Well I was a bit tired having not slept a wink but off I went, into the unknown. I had talked about doing the walk for weeks so there was no going back.

Three Hundred Miles Away ©

2007

My wife is asleep in bed,
three hundred miles away,
I am waiting,
for the start, of another day.

A long long way away from my love,
asleep, in our bed,
I wish I could lay my head.
The attraction keeps on calling me,
inside is a place where I want to be ,
with my love,
I long to lay my head.

Three hundred miles away,
waiting for the sun to light the day,

I'm in North Queensferry,
the bridge looks silently awake
silently awake I'd say,
silently awake
some three hundred miles away

Quiet Like in North Queensferry ©

2010

Wheest! On th' wend at North Queensferry,
where I chose to pause.
Quiet like in North Queensferry,
surveying surroundings because.
I'm drawn by a self-seeking search
early hours I respect,
man and his mettle did they bury
by the Forth in North Queensferry?

Steadfast the bridge a Victorian bequest,
a task men dangerously done.
Withstanding the elements of winter,
saturated in the summer sun.

Soon there'll be a sound
North Queensferry has heard before,
those behind drawn curtains
inside closed door.
Steel upon steel
wheels on rails,
North Queensferry hasn't woken yet
but I bet she can tell some tails.

Stories of man, sweat and blood labouring long,
a bustling bar a beer and a song.
What went to plan today,
and curse in a foul mouthing way,
what went damn wrong!

North Queensferry hasn't spoken yet
but I bet she has heard every word.
Notable buildings,
witnessed industrial endurance
photo-graphical assurance.

Man and his mettle of that age,
and their venturous quest to earn a wage.

One day there was a sound
North Queensferry hadn't heard before.
Steel upon steel
wheels on rails,
North Queensferry
afore I'm gone c'mon and tell some tales.

Wheest! On th' wend at North Queensferry,
where I chose to rest.
Quiet like in North Queensferry
Wheest! My self-order of respect

Later I was to research into the building of the Forth Rail
Bridge and although it was and still is a magnificent
construction there were fatalities. It was in 2013 that I first
saw the monuments either side of the bridge in North and
South Queensferry.

In 2008 there was a post from a lady by the name of May of
Scotland's Enchanted Kingdom, stating that she has a
particular interest in the Forth Rail Bridge as her Gt
Grandfather was one of the men who helped build it. He
was to survive but May added that it is still a tragedy with

so many men who lost their lives building the magnificent bridge.

Thomas Joseph Harris ©

2008

You must have visualised the manufacturing construction,
Advancing young man beyond toiling day introduction.
How many summers had passed since your day in school?
Secure in class at your desk on a bench or stool.

You entered into a world of earning a wage,
Nuts bolts and drawings of steelwork design on a page.
Thomas Joseph Harris,
That morn, were you looking ahead?
Or was the warmth of the shawl inviting you to laze in bed.
Thomas Joseph Harris, what could have been?
If you had lived beyond sixteen.

Did you ever conceive the Forth Bridge a legacy of your day?
I'm sorry young sir I deplore it ended that way.

Thomas Joseph Harris,
Your short life I am respecting.
Weren't you the first that died?
Or does research of mine need correcting.
Too young to leave a widow of a wife,
Thomas Joseph Harris,
…Weren't you the first to lose your life?

How many summers had passed since your day in school?
Secure in class at your desk on a bench or stool.
Thomas Joseph Harris, you never reached your prime.
If no bard has valued your worth, I deem it is time.

Thomas Joseph Harris
Aged 16
Storekeeper / Clerk
Forth Rail Bridge

Fell into the Forth and drowned
27/11/1883

Accordingly there was a loss of 98 men who came from far and wide to labour on this magnificent structure of its age. Public Houses in the vicinity of the two anchoring points at North and South Queensferry had to be prepared for the end of shift.

Grab o' Th' Glass ©

2007

Hard skinned hands of the working man,
fabrication fit to plan.
Labouring high as the wind was blowing,
day by day the bridge kept growing.
O'er the Firth of Forth, linking south to the north.

When working sound was dulled,
hundreds of pints were about to be pulled.
Hammers and spanners went clickity clank
hundreds of pints are about to be drank.

The end of the shift men were gagging,
a brew and a smoke they'll be fagging.
Hundreds of pints are pulled and ready,
on the long bar to be drunk.
They entered in mass, with a grab o' th' glass,
hundreds of pints were sunk.

Day by day the bridge kept growing,
it kept on growing, the men kept going,
it kept on growing from 1883,
it kept on, kept on growing

The view of the bridge and the Forth was majestic. It led me to think about my young days in the 1960s and Millers Bridge in Dixon Street, not far from Monmore Green. I can recall the old bridge being replaced by the one that's still there today. When cycling to school I had to carry my bike over the footbridge to the other side, it seemed an eternity before the bridge was functional. These bridges and their stature are incomparable but I couldn't help but do so. The canal at Millers Bridge was an opening to another world for me, my imaginative mind worked overtime, the tow paths were a history lesson in themselves and something that cannot be taught in a classroom. The evidence of the hard work of man and horse was all around. I would run my fingers down the grooves in the brickwork that had been cut by ropes pulled by horses towing barges.

The weather that morning was bright and sunny and I arrived at Burntisland railway station just before 10am. My plan was to catch the train back to North Queensferry to collect my car. When returning to the station car park, where I had arrived earlier that morning and parked as a lone driver, I noticed that it was now full with other commuters' vehicles. Before leaving North Queensferry I spent a short while at the Forth Rail Bridge. The chef from the nearby Albert Hotel took a couple of photos of me wearing my newly purchased Black Country "Tay Shirt".

When getting close to the bridge and witnessing its enormous size you understand why it is so famous. What a great legacy those men from the Victorian age left behind. I have read that many men came from all over Europe to work on the bridge, starting in 1879. Perhaps there was a Black Country man or two who toiled on that great engineering feat. Their labouring day and night produced a structure that became a symbol of Scotland. There were fatalities during the seven years it took to build the bridge and I believe the first person to lose his life was a boy of sixteen.

I couldn't have selected a better place for my base than the Beach House at Burntisland. This was built in 1860 and was formerly a Victorian tea-room. It was, as named, next to the beach and the views from my bedroom window were magnificent, in the distance I could see the city of Edinburgh and in the Forth was the Isle of Inchkeith.

The Fife Coastal Path passed outside the door and the railway line was directly behind the building and the trains that went past periodically added to its character. On the other side of the railway line was a green belt of land called The Links and every summer crowds gather there to watch the Highland games.

After lunch I set off again along the coast path heading for Kirkcaldy, the birthplace of my dad's real mother, named Kennedy. On the coast road near Pettycur Bay is a memorial where the last Celtic King was killed.

I walked into Kirkcaldy via the beach and I could see the floodlights of Raith Rovers Football Club. I purchased a pin badge and was given a pen for my efforts of my day's walk starting back at the Forth Bridge in the early hours. I was disappointed to find the house where my Kennedy's lived had been demolished for re-development. An hour later I caught the bus from Kirkcaldy back to Burntisland and the Beach House.

At breakfast the next morning I was listening to the
landlady's daughter playing the piano before going to
school. She played the "Skye Boat Song" as I sat and looked
out at the Isle of Inchkeith, the tune fitting the moment.

I drove to Pathhead to park up and walk the next stretch of
the coast path. The weather was glorious and I could see for
miles along the coastline. The towns began to change the
further east I walked. Dysart was lovely as were West and
East Wemyss. I noticed a small five-a-side football pitch
overlooking the land's end and I wondered how many
footballs had been kicked out of play and floated out into
the Forth to be brought back by the tide further along the
coast.

Upon the cliff edge there was a couple admiring the view across the Forth. I politely asked the man if he would take a photograph of me. "Are you from Birmingham?" he asked. "No," I replied, "Wolverhampton." At that point my mobile phone rang so I wasn't sure if I'd correctly heard what the man said next as I thought he had told me that his mother came from Wolverhampton. I had heard correct and she was born on the Dudley Road. What a small world it is, I thought as the man told me about his relations in Bloxwich and Wednesfield and about a pub in Kingswinford with low ceilings.

Along my final stretch of the coastal path I could see to my left the Lomond Hills, a good 12 miles away. I stopped for a while to admire the view. From my dad's village of Ladybank you can see the hills quite clearly and I was put in mind of one of my earlier poems about my father's childhood.

When walking into Buckhaven on Tuesday lunch time I came across a war memorial. The monument was at least 25 feet high and on the top was a statue of a soldier standing proud, with the Firth of Forth in the background. I always take time to read the names of those that fell for our freedom. I couldn't help but notice the surname of Anderson a few times. This is a name that is in both lines of my Bennet and Kennedy Fife roots.

Ian Understands ©

2007

Ian will understand,
In villages and towns
All over this land.
Memorial names on view.
Brothers, sons and fathers,
And husbands too.
Where did they come from?
Where did they die?
Ian understands,
Why I don't hurry by.
Artefact and skills
Of a craftsman's hands.
Why should we read it?
Ian understands.
A sacrificial life, a soldier and his name,
In a village or a town
From whence they came.
Where did they come from?
Where did they die?
Ian understands,
Why I don't hurry by.

The primary stage of this poem was written at a memorial
in Buckhaven, Fife.
15 May 2007

From the memorial at Buckhaven I walked down to
Bayview, the home of East Fife Football Club, a superb little
ground by the coast. I noticed two men talking by a tractor
and trailer, by an open corner gate. They told me they were
the groundsmen and allowed me to take a look inside at the
pitch. It was in fine condition considering it was the end of
the season. The men were maintaining the line where the
assistant referees run up and down. By the main reception
area I was invited by an executive of the club to enter the
pitch via the players' tunnel. I found everyone at East Fife
very friendly and a credit to Scottish football. The young
lady in reception directed me to the bus station, crossing the
Bawbee Bridge at Leven, where I browsed around the shops
for a while before boarding a bus back to Pathhead where I
had left my car. Just over the road from the sands by
Ravenscraig Castle is a pub called The Path and I thought it
would be an appropriate place to sample a refreshing pint
in celebration of walking part of the coastal path.

On returning to the Beach House at Burntisland late that
afternoon I dipped my feet into the ice cold water of the
Firth of Forth. I didn't play for Ladybank Violet as in my
poem but writing that poem had inspired me to come here.
Having lived a Wulfrunian way all my life my two days
walking in Fife gave me great satisfaction. In my own way I
felt I had balanced the books of my family's divide.

91

I travelled home that Tuesday evening, thinking of what I had achieved and wishing that my dad could have known. All the places I had walked through he would have known growing up. Earlier that day I had walked past a chap working on his lorry within 100 yards of the Forth. I imagined my dad doing just the same if he had stayed in Fife. I remember Dad taking my brother Gareth and me to yards in Derry Street and Steelhouse Lane, where he worked on cars and lorries when we were kids.

I arrived home late that evening and took off my Scotland rugby top and my Black Country Tay Shirt, that I had worn all trip, and put them in the wash basket. On my shirt I had chosen the saying of "Ow Bin yer?" I bin great, mate! Just a wee bit tired now."

When I Walked To Leven ©

2007

I arrived at the Forth Bridge at the break of dawn,
On May 14th on an early morn.
By the 15th I'd walked into Leven,
On paths and beaches and trails uneven.
No dismal clouds were brewing a wee shower,
I saw silver sands at Aberdour.
Edinburgh I viewed from Lammerlaws,
Castle ruins by rocky shores.
The bluest sky I had ever seen,
Over Burntisland way beyond Aberdeen.
In the Lang Toun of Kirkcaldy,
Links Street I was conscious of a kindred stroll.
West and East Wemyss were peaceful and quiet,
Also Michaels Colliery of coal.
There's no more working mine I found,
Silent shafts are underground.
No coal soot faces in lantern light,
In miner's hands to aid their sight.
I observed a memorial for Methil and Buckhaven,
They sailed from these shores washed and clean-shaven.
Taking time to respect the gallant who fell.
And died for this land in wars of bloody hell.
I imagined them all as I walked to Bayview.

Fishermen, Weavers and Miners too,

Were they shattered and buried in a far foreign soil?

In the mills and the fields did their widows still toil?

Onwards from the Parish of Methil I strode,

The thought of kilted soldiers lessoned my load.

I felt rays of the sun tanning my skin,

How do I start, how can I begin.

To explain my emotions by all of those shores,

That fantastic view from Lammerlaws.

Those paths and beaches and trails uneven,

The Bawbee Bridge when I walked into Leven.

With a small piece of stone that fit in my hand,

That I had picked from the beach at Pathhead sand.

Another two days fascinated by Fife,

My ancestral Kingdom is alive in my life.

I was to draw back and still do on memories of that time in my life. Just looking at pictures and adding new paragraphs to my story raises many feelings. It was a personal challenge that I never thought possible. There was plenty of emotions especially whilst resting in Burntisland as I was in a seaside resort.

In between the journey of walking from Burntisland to Leven, I had to catch the train back to collect my car at North Queensferry Station. I felt lonely and guilty by the sands and wondered to myself if I had been selfish with my Fife Coastal Path desire. We had recently became Grandparents for the first time and there was a call inside telling me that I should be back at home. Then suddenly out of the blue a fellow spoke to me.

It is noticeable when in Fife how friendly people are. Never do I pass anyone on the coast without them acknowledging me and always willing to take up a conversation. Whenever they hear what I'm there for they always give me chapter and verse of the area. Fifer's do seem friendlier to strangers but it may be my imagination.

A couple of people in walking boots and chatting injected my passion once again and I was soon on the path to Kirkcaldy and beyond.

A Friendly Fifer Said "Hello" ©

2007

Mid-day in May in Burntisland,
Absorbing the warmth of the weather,
Fife and I were alone together.
The sun made it all worthwhile,
After a treacherous journey,
Many a lonely rainy wet mile.
The preceding eve I had said my farewell,
To my comfortable abode of family personnel.

Sky was quite clear and the Forth was near,
Sand was gold dust in my hand.
The Isle of Inchkeith I cast my eyes,
I listened inside to homecoming cries.
I'm soon to rise and stride out some more,
Into the unknown by the shore.
Absorbing the warmth of the weather,
Fife and I were alone together.
As I was lost in what time I should go,
A friendly Fifer said "hello."

Feelings kept on coming and going and what was an easy
task of travelling to Fife to walk the coastal path appeared
not to be. Simply because it was too far away to arrange and
our normal summer holiday had to be planned. Gone was
the plan of walking it all in 2007 but at the very least I had
memories in mind and a memento or two.

Did Alexander Kennedy
Walk This Way? ©

2007

Maybe, perhaps, I wonder,
Alexander was here on Pathhead sand.
At Ravenscraig Castle high over the shore,
About the year 1864.

Did he walk like me, by the sea?
Down steps to the waters edge of this land,
Alexander, I have a stone from Pathhead sand.

Did Alexander Kennedy walk this way?
Today, tomorrow or yesterday.
Alexander, to Dysart did he then roam?
Away from his Kennedy family home.
Perhaps he would have looked like me, out to sea,
From the castle high over this land,
Alexander, I have a stone from Pathhead sand.

Alexander Kennedy where did you walk?
What did you look like how did you talk?
Wherever I'm going have you been there before?
About the year 1864.
Ravenscraig Park in the coastal woodland,
Held affectionately in my hand,
Alexander, I have a stone from Pathhead sand.

I instantly noticed the view of the sunrise in Kirkcaldy and pulled my car over to stop and take some pictures. It was just past 6.30am and what a magnificent scene, it was then that I knew it had been worth the long night drive from my home in Codsall, just outside Wolverhampton.

It was early on Sunday morning 16th March 2008 when I arrived back in the Kingdom of Fife to walk the second stage of the Coastal Path. The previous May I had walked for 2 days starting at the Forth Rail Bridge and ending at Leven bus station about 30 miles around the coast. I had decided to walk the path around the coast of Fife because this is where my Scottish ancestry lies and I feel a strong connection there. With every passing year I learn a little bit more about Fife and after today I will have seen and learned even more. It seemed strange driving through Burntisland where I had stayed on my last visit. I was familiar with the roads and the area and coastal memories came flooding back. When I passed near to the Beach House, the guest house where I had stayed, I looked for the Saltire flag that flew from the roof that had caught my attention on my first visit. I had a good idea where my guest house was in Leven and headed there to park my car in the street near by. When I arrived there I stopped outside the church over the road. Then I noticed there was a church almost next door then another one down the road.

I headed for the beach down by the power station at 7.20am and was soon walking. The question was could I get to Crail by mid afternoon? It was just over 20 miles away but what kind of terrain would it be and how is my fitness. I had not walked a good distance in many months.

The dark coastline was sweeping away to my right and it looked a long way away to be walking. The sky was changing every other minute as the morning was unfolding into what would become a fine day.

The Silver Trail to Crail ©

2008

Silver shone o'er the Forth from under a blanket of grey,
This morn in March, the last time I was here it was May.

Early once more by the sensuous shore
Onward I gather my trail,
Twenty so miles over sand steps and styles
Walking from Leven to Crail.

In the Kingdom am I and silver is mine,
In a dawning that's so divine.
Unnoticed by the lazy eye,
In the Kingdom, so proud I could cry.

Impressed by viaducts at Largo
Mount Pleasant a rainbow's apparent,
Beaming and gleaming beyond where I had been
Sadly becoming transparent.

Navigating the climb around Ruddons Point,
Testing my muscles and an aging joint.
Ruins near St Monans the chapel at the edge,
My footsteps were careful along the ledge.
Beneath the headstones as they lay in rest,

Respectful am I in my quest.
Who faces the sea and the Isle of May,
As I link the two bridges of the Forth and Tay,

Dwellings near seawalls in Pittenween
Oh how active it must have been,
Along the East Neuk coastal places
The excitement and fear in fishermen's faces.
Portraying there worth in a museum display,
Mans challenge of survival of yesterday.

The harbour walk to Anstruther
Pittenweem a desire to quench my thirst,
In the Larachmhor with a glass of ale
Then onward once more on the trail to Crail.
Stepping on stones and footprints in sand,
Walking my walk on this land.
It will be for every ancestral life,
That was born and toiled in the Kingdom of Fife.

Blue sky o'er the Forth from under pillows of white,
This March afternoon Crail became in sight.
Unnoticed by the lazy eye,
In the Kingdom, so proud I could cry.

Th' Shores o' Fife ©

2009

Sparkle o' th' salty sea, artistically attracting me,
Pursuing life there on th' shores o' Fife.

Land for miles seems endlessly I walk and wander tirelessly,
Pursuing life there on th' shores o' Fife.
The bays and braes along th' shores o' Fife

Occasionally an abandoned home I stumble on as I roam,
Pursuing life there on th' shores o' Fife.

A separate time an equal place a person with a different
face,
Pursuing life there on th' shores o' Fife.
The bays and braes along th' shores o' Fife

Irresponsibly birds they fly spectacularly, aggressively,
Pursuing life there on th' shores o' Fife.

Wildlife always close at hand little footprints in the sand,
Pursuing life there on th' shores o' Fife.
The bays and braes along th' shores o' Fife

This feast thereby upon this earth increased existence and
my worth,
Pursuing life there on th' shores o' Fife.

Am I foolish with my honesty to share this joy with thee?
Pursuing life there on th' shores o' Fife.
The bays and braes along th' shores o' Fife

Ocean choreography, exciting fighting strife,
Pursuing life there on th' shores o' Fife.

Ay it's grand there on th' shores o' Fife.

Many times, because of my roots, I have researched the history of Fife. I remember learning that a Celtic goalkeeper had died through injuries suffered in a game and was buried there.
When a Chelsea goalkeeper was injured in the season of 2006-07 in similar circumstances, it revived the Celtic goalkeepers tragic event.

I decided to write my poem about John Thomson and researched his sad story. I found that in some reports he was born in Kirkcaldy and in others in Cardenden, both in Fife, they were at least in the same area. I also wanted to be factually correct as possible with his final resting place. Was it Cardenden or Bowhill so I surfed the internet to find the correct address of Bowhill Cemetery to be in Cardenden.

In my research I was attracted to all reports of those who had walked the 55 miles from Glasgow to Fife, sleeping at night on the Crags. There was born the start of my poem for John Thomson.

Quite often I came across Tom Greig's book, My Search For Celtic's John and decided to purchase it after I had written my poem. In reading his book he was also attracted to this tragic story and is now considered as an expert with his book being a great read. What was also most interesting was that it is advertised as a 'must have' if you have a connection to Fife.

Upon reading Tom Greig's book to date, my poem of John Thomson appears to be quite factually correct.

Within a few days I had the main lines or and verses but not in the context that I wanted. I 'juggled' them around until I was satisfied as I could possibly be. One line I could not settle on until I thought of, 'A journey for John's courageous saves,' I only vaguely knew of John's story and did not know the man in depth until Petr Cech's injury for Chelsea. But most certainly I love the game he died for, Fife where he was born and Scotland he represented.

In March 2008 I called in at Bowhill Cemetery on route home from Leven after walking the second part of the Fife Coastal Path. I wanted to see the final resting place of John Thomson and to pay my respect to the 'Laddie frae Cardenden.'

They Walked All The Way From Glasgow ©

2006

Scotland and Celtic's Prince of Goalkeepers

John Thomson

1909-1931

They knew they had to be there,

They had little time to prepare.

Some walked all the way from Glasgow,

With bonnets, scarves and flowers.

They walked all the way from Glasgow,

They carried their gifts for hours.

111

They slept all night on the Crags,
A wee bit of grub in their bags.
They had little time to prepare,
All they knew was they had to be there.

A keeper of goal was John Thomson
In his prime with the utmost respect,
This challenge he made was fatal
His goal he was trying to protect.
For a handful of leather not hitting the net,
The young still listen and never forget.
An Old Firm game in bygone time,
He died defending his line.

The game of football was physically stunned,
His club and his country did mourn.
Some walked all the way from Glasgow,
To Fifeshire where he was born.
A journey for John's courageous save,
For a hand full of leather an early grave.

They buried John Thomson in his native land
Musicians from the Bowhill Pipe and the Silver Band,
Led the procession that day
Through the crowded streets they made their way.
They came from afar and they stood there in awe

They looked at the sky
They stared at the floor,
The year was 1931
But his story never grows old,
Each generation hears of the sad tale
Every day a new listener is told.

Near Cardenden lies a religious brave man,
His courage merits this praise.
This mining community witnessed the grief,
One of footballs tragic sad days.

Celtic v Rangers
Ibrox
5 September 1931
John Thomson died after diving at the feet of Rangers
forward Sam English.
The epitaph on John Thomson's gravestone,
'They never die who live in the hearts they leave behind'

A few weeks later I was back on the road to Fife, this time with my wife and both our Mothers. I enjoyed showing them places that I had walked through and stayed at in my earlier visits. I was already gaining knowledge and my enthusiasm for Fife was evident. I was recalling where I had rested and places of interest were being pointed out. It was good to have family with me and not far away on this stage of the coastal path. What was pleasing is that my mom was to be in Ladybank (dad's village) where she had never been.

We were booked into the Craws Nest in Anstruther and spent a good few hours looking around the harbour and resort known for its fishing history. I skipped my breakfast next morning to get to Crail at dawn to start my 3rd stage. I parked up on the road overlooking the harbour and made my way down to the coast. I was greeted by an amazing sunrise that must be part of everyday life here on the east coast of Scotland.

Another main pilgrim route to St Andrews is along the East Coast and here I was treading in age-old footsteps of thousands of pilgrims preceding me. I was heading to Fife Ness, the most eastern point of Fife where it has a Coastguard station. I received a good morning wave from an officer who looked like he was heading for home after his night shift. There were signs of it being a fishing settlement in former times.

The path passes Constantine's Cave where the King was killed c874. It then becomes rugged and challenging and getting to St Andrews was like trying to pull in a great white shark with a 2-bob fishing rod brought from a second hand stall on Bilston Market.

There was a change of direction to north west and towards Cambo Sands where for the first time this morning I was to speak to another who was out walking her dog. She kindly took a photo of me and was amused when I told her I needed proof that I had been here. Greenkeepers were busy on the golf course and a friendly wave was sent my way. I was nearing Kingsbarns and then Boarhills where I believe to have an ancestral connection in both places on my Kennedy side but not of that name.

On my mind was that I am a Great Grandson of Isabella, born in Shorehead, St Andrews. On the East Sands she must have played many times and here am I 'walking ower the brae'.

St Andrews I'm On My Way ©

2008

Sleepy eyed and satisfied
East Neuk at early morn,
As an April day is born.

St Andrews I'm on my way,
I shall be with you later today.
This Great Grandson in Shorehead by the East Sand,
She did nae know I'd be striding out in this land.
Isabella, imagine yesteryear that someday
I'd come walking ower th' brae,

The Forth is a picture as the sun begins to rise,
Birth of day arrives before my eyes.
This joyous man it does impress,
Heading for the naval point at Fife Ness.

St Andrews I'm on my way,
I shall be with you later today.
Afore then there is many a sight to see,
Breeding, feeding and satisfying me.

Cambo Sands a solitary feel,
Serenity, it all seems so unreal.

The rugged coastline challenged my resistance,
Posts and walls they aided my assistance.
Isabella, where you're frae, for thine and thee,
My blood, body and mind is what I gie.

St Andrews I'm on my way,
I shall be with you later today.
One more set of steps to climb,
Fortifying on foretime.

This Great Grandson in Shorehead by the East Sand,
With you in mind and Fife in my heart and hand.

Isabella, imagine yesteryear that someday,
I'd come walking ower th' brae.

The sight of St Andrews lifted my spirit as I strode over Kinkell Braes through a caravan site. I was greatly impressed by the locality and the views of this site. This would lead to Lynne and I having a few holidays here in years that followed.

I was mighty proud of myself for thinking of walking the coastal path not knowing what personal satisfaction it would bring. To walk over the brae, onto East Sands and into the arms of my awaiting ancestors was the thought.

The Bonnie Bonnie Sand of St Andrews Bay ©

2006

As the sun shone over this glorious land,
I walked by the brine on the bonnie bonnie sand.
'Twas the breeze that whispered…
"Stand by here and gaze",
I was caught and captured by the wash of the wave.
I stood there in reverence transfixed for a while,
I was caught and captured as in a pretty girls smile.
When finding a love your heart will call,
If you stand and admire you will finally fall.
'Twas the breeze that whispered…
"Stand by here and gaze",
I was caught and captured by the wash of the wave.
Caught in the glory of this part of land,
Captured by the brine
And the bonnie bonnie sand.

It always embarrasses and amuses Lynne whenever I ask complete strangers to take our photo. If I warn her what I am going to do she insists that I don't. This picture with 'The Bonnie, Bonnie Sands' in the background was taken by a couple who were also amused by my asking.

In the background are the sands where they filmed Chariots of Fire. I have strolled around here many times with and without Lynne by either walking the path or on my early morning exercise. We have also been in that car-park on a rainy evening eating chips as the windows steamed up. Next evening we were to stay with friends Mark and Maggie in Edinburgh as he was Assistant Manager at Hibs.

It was good to see not only them but their teenage children who we can remember the day that they were born. They may have had no idea who these pair of Codsalites were but could tell by their parents that we were friends.

Back to that special holiday in Fife when Lynne and I were fortunate to take our mothers along. We visited Falkland on our last day but the Palace was closed and we could not wait the extra 2 hours as we were on the long road home.

Falkland Was Lovely
Oh Aye ©

2008

It was April it was, it was April oh aye,
Falkland was lovely I testify.
It was lovely it was, it was lovely oh aye,
Falkland was lovely oh aye.

Falkland literally often appears,
In chapters of Scotland's historic years.
The palace I picture at the gatehouse front,
Kings and Queens arriving to hunt.
Imprisoned was David the throne he was heir,
Robert III his son he died there.
In suspicious circumstances,
In a palace you imagine fine splendour dances.
I am always attracted to a market square,
Bruce fountain I study standing there,
East Lomond and buildings strive for attention
Architecture is ample and well worth a mention.
Wandering down a cobbled wynd,
Quaint wee shops and Inns I find.

It was April it was, it was April oh aye,
Falkland was lovely oh ay

Almost 12 months to the day that I had first started walking the coastal path I drove away from my home in Codsall. It was 11.15pm on a Tuesday evening and I wanted to be in St Andrews at dawn to start the fourth and final stage. As I pulled away from my house I felt a strong presence of my dad knowing what I was doing.

Bang on 6.00am I arrived at St Andrews East Sands. There was a cold brisk breeze as I laced my boots, locked my car and headed for the Tay Bridge, 19 or so miles away. I passed the Cathedral and Castle ruins and down to the famous Old Course where the groundsmen were busy. Most importantly and what I did not know at the time was that I walked passed my ancestors final place of rest.

This stage I found was less coastal than the others. I followed a home made coastal path sign and got lost having to backtrack and pick up the route. This put another hour and extra unnecessary miles onto my already blistered feet. I watched as planes were taking off at Leuchars Airfield. You could hear them for half a minute before seeing them appear from out of the trees and into the air.

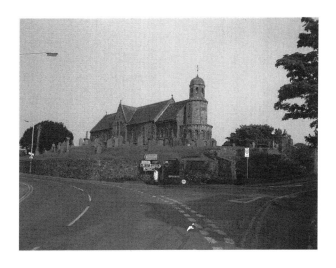

Finding Fife was life changing for me and soon I was to be up there as often as possible. I had received three or four invitations to be featured on Scotland or Fife websites and a mention or two in local newspapers. My poem Kingdom of Fife actually made the Fife Leader in 2003.

My writing mind was soon back and busy as Fife had given me great inspiration. I tended to revisit the Coastal path in mind and body to draft other work.

I looked over the Tay to Broughty Ferry at Tentsmuir Point while walking the Fife Coastal Path from St Andrews to Dundee. I recalled that it was the birthplace of Francis Munro who Wolves had brought from Aberdeen in 1968. I would then be a lad of 14 and remembered that Wolves were the 'Yankee Champions' the previous year. They beat Aberdeen 6-5 in the final and Munro had scored a hat trick against them. He came to Wolverhampton for a fee in the region of £55,000 giving them 9 years service as a cultured centre back.

Munro o' Broughty Ferry ©

2009

Ower th' Tay to Broughty Ferry,
A name I throw, Francis Munro.
Tentsmuir to Tayport I take a mo,
I take a mo and think of Frank Munro.

Munro o' Broughty Ferry,
Good? Aye he was very.
Consider I would as sacrilege
If forgetting I should nearing the Tay Road Bridge.

When Wolves were winners for Los Angeles,
An opposing performance was sure to please.
Scored three, did he for Washington Whips,
Munro, the name on Ronnie Allen's lips.

Munro o' Broughty Ferry,
He made the faithful merry.
Th' Dons o' Pittodrie to Molineux,
Francis, your service I am thanking you.

Francis, foregoing beside the Tay
Tayport to Dundee I'll be on my way,

With blistered feet I'm thinking of you
Yer 'auld Boss' Eddie Turnbull he liked you too.

So you folk there in Broughty Ferry,
I'll have you know that we loved Frank Munro.
Munro o' Broughty Ferry,
Good? Aye he was very.
Broughty Ferry ower th' Tay,
Fare ye weel I'm on ma wey.

Francis Michael Munro 25/10/1947 – 16/08/2011

Little did I know at the time of resting outside the Bell Rock
Tavern to grease my feet, that Tayport (Ferry-port-on-
Craig) had such an ancestral connection that was to surface
a few years later.

I carried on through aside the Tay with the Bridge getting
closer and closer. I felt relaxed, tired and excited and
engaged in conversation with every passing person. One
was a fellow from the north of England who had a boat up
here as he loved the Tay.

Dundee was a terrific sight as was the sparkling Tay, the end was near. I walked over the bridge with a sea breeze that cut through my skin. There was a reason for me to be here and I knew it, proving that there is more to life than where you were born.

My Scottish ancestry walk was over and I hobbled painfully
along the streets of Dundee to the bus station at Seagate
(address of GGG Grandfather James Brown on the 1881
census plus Bennet in 1861). I now needed to get back to
my car at St Andrews and drive to my guest house at Lundin
Links in the East Neuk. It was the evening of the Champions
League Final in 2008 between Chelsea and Manchester
United. John Terry slipped whilst taking a crucial penalty, I
wasn't to know as I was exhausted and fell asleep hearing
the news at 4.00am next morning.

I was to realise later that my story started the previous year with mentioning Aaron, our first grandchild. Since then we have had Liam, another grandson and cousin to Aaron. They were on my mind on my journey back to St Andrews. I wondered if one day they would read my story or perhaps want to see Fife for themselves. If they don't ever come to Fife where they have an ancestry connection they will at least be able to look at a map and see where the Forth and Tay Bridges are and know where I have walked. A couple of bonnie grandaughters, Kiera-Marie and cousin Caitlyn were here in the following two years as we entered into the next stage of our life.

From This Window Fife I See ©

2008

This wee proud piece of Bonnie Scotland,
The copious coast I've walked along.
This wee proud piece of Bonnie Scotland,
A feeling for the Kingdom grows strong.

He found love but relinquished plenty,
When National Service called.

His name and connection with the Kingdom,
I've re-established and also re-installed.

Dad, if you knew what I had done,
Me, your second son.
I wish I could turn back precious time,
You'd be here in this land that's more yours than mine.
Sadly for me it cannot be,
I desire for satisfaction not someone's sympathy.
Dad, if you knew what I had done,
Me, your second son.

I've embraced and cherished roots in Fife,
Too late to share with you in life.
Dad, from this window Fife I see,
Yesterday I walked into Dundee.

St Andrews 6.00am I started early in the day.
Step by step to the bridge at 3.00pm I crossed the Tay,
Dad, if you knew what I had done.
Me, your second son.

This wee proud piece of Bonnie Scotland,
The copious coast I've walked along.
This wee proud piece of Bonnie Scotland,
A feeling for the Kingdom grows strong.

The Forth Rail Bridge to Leven,
From Leven to the harbour at Crail.
Crail then on to St Andrews,
Four times to the Kingdom I came to prevail.

Dad, from this window Fife I see,
Yesterday I walked into Dundee.
Dad, if you knew what I had done.
Me, your second son.

From this window Fife I see,
Satisfied that I have walked from North Queensferry to
Dundee.
Dad, if you knew what I had done.
Me, …. …… …

The remainder of 2008 was a satisfying year and my photographs were placed into albums in order of the day. Once my blistered feet had healed I was thinking of what else I could do to embrace Fife in a challenging way. My biggest problem was having the time to do whatever I decided but quite frankly the coastal path had everything that I wished for.

What had happened was that I had became familiar with the coastal villages and wanted to return to show my wife and hopefully others. Nevertheless the following year was 2009 and that meant it was homecoming and there was a good enough reason to have to come back.

Homecoming Scotland 2009 was an events programme to celebrate 250 years since the birth of Robert Burns. It was for Scot's or of Scottish descent or just love Scotland, a celebration of Scotland's contribution to the world.

You Keep On Singing Scotland ©

Homecoming Scotland 2009

Temperature plummeted last night
Aye, it was cold this morning
Out door had a bit of a bite
The sun though in the window is warming

Spring growth of grass on the back lawn
A wee bit thicker each day
Soon the light will be lingering longer
And soon I'll be wanting away

You keep on singing Scotland
You sing so clear
You keep on singing Scotland
Louder year by year

The wanderer in me is conspicuous
Behaving and being suspicious
Cometh the time near the light night of May
Time I'll be wanting away

You keep on singing Scotland
Conserving my self counterpart
You keep on singing Scotland
Singing in my heart

The wanderer in me is awaking
Underlying let there be no mistaking
Wanderers shan't be inactive
Homecoming year is attractive

My Fife experience was playing havoc with my mind and
time spent reading and writing was plenty. So much so that
I dreamt this one night that my dad was on the floor by my
bed and I told him what I had done and all the places I had
been. He sat there without saying a word and smiled. Of
course it did not happen but it was there in my mind and
remained so.

He Was There With Me Last Night©

2009

He was there with me last night
All be it in a dream,
I told him what I'd done
I told him where I'd been.

I saw a surprising smile
A satisfying look,
Although it didn't happen
All is fine there in my book

I started to take in the north coast of Fife more as I liked the view over to Dundee and beyond. The very fact that you are by the Tay brings one into a sad day in rail history. It is a strange feeling when standing by the Tay Rail Bridge in Fife and seeing the stumps in the water of the first bridge. Imagining that fated evening of 28th December 1879 when the bridge collapsed during a wretched storm. There was no survivors from the train that fell into the wintry Tay. Bella Neish, aged 5 of Lochee was travelling with her father that evening.

Bella's Lament ©

2009

Bella were you Bonny,
were you the apple of an eye?
Oh bonny Bella,
I hear your mother cry.

Tell Me o' The Tay ©

2011

Tell me o' Balmerino Abbey
remains, ruined and grey
tell me heritage
Tell me o' the Tay

Tell me odes
tell me o' meadows, snowdrops and roads
tell me o' water o'er the way
Tell me o' the Tay

Tell me all its worth
this wide expansive rippling firth
sun shines on the southern shore today
Tell me o' the Tay

Tell me 'bout the Tay
tell me bits of everything, anything,
like seals that swim and birds that wing
effortless o'er the Tay
Tell me o' the Tay

Tell me o' whalers
and Dundee Sailors
they who sailed her way
Tell me o' the Tay

Tell me 'bout the Tay
where her wares they went away
hold and sold her wares away
Tell me o' the Tay

Tell me tails of masts and sails
daydreamers, Paddle Steamers
local news, a Sunday cruise
Tell me o' the Tay

Tell me o' Balmerino Abbey
and monks there o' that day
tell me o' the harbour
Tell me o' the Tay

Tell me 'bout the Tay
tell me how lovely, when the Discovery
came home to the Tay
Tell me o' the Tay

An early May morning 2010 in the parish of Falkland the
church clock chimed six times as I walked from my car.
Once again I had travelled overnight to Fife, crossing the
border about 3.00am, this time to climb the Lomonds. I had
first mentioned them in my poem The Kingdom of Fife and I
wanted to see for myself how good the views were from up
there so I was hoping for a clear morning. I hadn't done the
best of homework and wasn't sure where the best place to
park my car would be for an easy access. I did find it a bit
hard, as it is quite a short and steep climb from Falkland
taking about an hour. I found myself damning Scotland for
drawing me to challenges like this, as I'm not getting any
younger. Far gone was the time when I was running
marathon after marathon. The only real exercise I get these

147

days are the daily dog walk and a 20 minute work out at home before I set off to work.

With a fast beating heart and tired legs I paused a few times to see the magnificent view that was appearing behind me. I was told that Hector Bennet, my Great Grandfather would sit outside his house in Monkstown, Ladybank admiring the Lomonds; I wanted to climb the Lomonds for that very reason. To be up where he has looked at countless times. I was cursing a bit because as I was getting close to the top that there was some cloud forming in a southern easterly direction and moving around the hill. If I had any gas left as they say I would have put my foot on it but to be honest I was shattered.

It was noticeable when I did get to the summit of just under 1,400ft that the wind was stronger the south side of East Lomond. The views from there over the Ballo and Harperleas Reservoirs were spectacular, well worth suffering for a while from aching joints and breathlessness. And guess what? I'd forgot to bring my camera so pictures taken from my mobile phone had to do.

Damn Ye Scotland ©

2010

I have to catch my breath
my heart is beating fast,
damn ye Scotland dam ye
the damning didnae last.

Drawn again to challenge
or peace of mind to come,
but damn ye Scotland dam ye
at this time it is nae fun.

Step, by step, in a rut, I put my sole of a shoe.
I cannae lie, oh my, o'er Fife there's a grand view.
Falkland up to East Lomond,
tough, for the age of this man,
if an eye is looking at East Lomond
on the peak of it, there I am.

A wee speck that's well out of breath
at this time it is nae fun.
damn ye Scotland dam ye
damn glad, I am, that I come.

From there I followed the trail passing disused quarries and down to Craigmead car park making my way by road back to Falkland. By this time I had recovered from the climb and was appreciating the tranquil sound of running water and birds singing. I was being looked on as suspicious by the ewes and their lambs in the field on the outskirts of Falkland. This wee trek really did ease the working stress of the past year. I decided to leave West Lomond about 1,700ft to some other time giving me a reason to pay Fife another visit.

Within a short while I walked into Kingskettle Cemetery and like a lot of places in Fife there is a fine view of the Lomonds. I read my ancestors gravestone, having only found it in recent years and thought about people I had never met. Certainly many times in their life they would have looked at the Lomonds, those two peaks of volcanic origin that dominate the skyline, and now I've been up there, what a feeling.

Next stop was Ladybank where I sat on a bench by the war memorial eating a sausage roll that I had purchased for breakfast. Soon I was driving south arriving back in Codsall about 2.30pm. In our dining room is a water coloured painting of the Lomonds by Leslie Broadfield, a relation of mine, from a photograph that I had taken. I have studied it many times and thought that I should climb up there.

Lomond Hills by Leslie Broadfield a Wolverhampton
relative of mine

I Love The Lomonds ©

2007

I wish I could see the Lomonds
Each morning when I rise,
I love the Lomonds
An impressive sight they are to my eyes.
The Lovely Lomonds
Their stature stands supreme,
In the picturesque Fife landscape scene.
The Lomonds sadly everyday
Are hundreds of miles away,
The Lomonds I then compromise
I see when I close my eyes.

Auld Dundee with Hector ©

2009

Hello Hector, Hector hello
you lived many miles away,
many years ago.
Hello Hector, 'how do ye do'
you loved the hillside view, I love it too.

Aye the Lomonds
this laddie has heard
making me climb them
and put into word

When a bairn oh Hector,
how was Dundee?
Dundee, you and me in the auld day
I wish we could be.

We'd watch the sunshine
sparkle the Tay,
the Law we shall clamber
one Dundee auld day.

Chimney's and textile mills
no finer city or town,

jute manufacturing
Dundee wore the crown.

Now then Hector
that was your time
imagining Hector
it's also mine

1880 Dundee
your father he worked on the ships,
did he ever go sailing
and have salt on his lips?

I'm looking on o'er
to the north coast of Fife,
watching you over
with your lady, your wife.

She came from St Andrews
a wee further along,
a Fisherman's daughter
did he sing her a Fishermen's song?

She worked in the mills
to earn her pay,

singing their songs
that they still sing today

You went away Hector,
away from Dundee,
on ferry or train, in snow, wind or rain
leave ye be the industrial identity?

Dundee whalers, drunken sailors
kept coming or going away,
the Town House oh Hector
I shall toast ye one day.

So long Hector, Hector so long
Dundee, you and me in the auld day,
join in with a Jute Weavers song
that they still sing sweet on the street,
but I'm dreaming oh Hector
for we never did meet.

The Town House, Dundee 2014,

"you may just see
Auld Rabbbie at the front door
o' The Town House in Dundee"

I'd had a lovely few hours this one day in July, talking to my mom that got me thinking later of my dad and how he pronounced certain Scots villages, involving my children and grandchildren in my thoughts and finding a forgotten poem then suddenly, in through the door of life, always runs a little one.

In Through The Door
Runs a Little One ©
2010

I've climbed your hills
those hills in your child eye,
and marked my skin,
to prove and show
that you, my old man as we say,
are within

I've climbed those hills
that you could see from your front window,
no one asked if I can,
this half English, Scottish man

Grabbing the existence of life
a personal opinion, I have done,

this Grandad, Father and Son
in hand it was heavy, thereon did I shoulder,
but didn't anticipate the obvious,
an age thing, growing older

I grabbed the horn
no question of where I was born,
respectful of what I had done
a personal opinion,
this Grandad, Father and Son

Looking at pictures
your Grandparents, that was a treat,
looking at someone
you probably didn't meet

But I'm looking in reality
at my Great Grandmother,
I'm looking at words
of a lost son, an uncle, a brother

What I'm seeing is time
passages of time,
paragraphs, chapters of time
stories of old, knowing little of yours,
combining with mine

The hills that I climbed
no one asked me if I can,
I just went there one morning
this half English, Scottish man

Now, my joy is more
in through the door runs a little one,
and I smile, this Grandad, Father and always your son
but very often dad, I get weary and cold
not expecting anything
but didn't anticipate the obvious
an age thing, growing old

In through the door runs a little one
and shows me that life does go on,
stating the obvious.....

HERE IN THE HOWE ©

2011

Oh, how leesome
the Howe and all its pasture
will it last yer? Oh Laddie
will it now

here in the Howe
a lang and lestie measure of
rural pleasure and a gladsome mark
a scar that hurts my heart
Bonnie Scotland
guilty thou art

oh, how welcome
the Howe and heritable history
a wee tait of mystery
here in the Howe

life that breathed
souls that grieved
folk, they travel by past yer
will it last yer? Oh Laddie
here in the Howe

Oh how awesome,
the twosome Lomonds
goad the road I chose
and those, who travel by past yer
I ask yer, will it last yer? Oh Laddie
will it now

will it last yer?
here in the evergreen heather
and mauve flowers
while away the hours
but now, do you want some more?
on to Luthrie and to Norman's Law

It was in 2008 that I wrote 'Auchtermuchty Fields', a fictitious poem about young love. This poem of mine is displayed on a popular Fife website. I was amazed to be complimented on the poem by a gentleman from Oklahoma City, USA. His great, great, grandfather was born in Auchtermuchty and left with his wife to Lower Canada in 1831. He really enjoyed my poem and it made him feel connected.

Auchtermuchty Fields ©

2008

He came from Auchtermuchty where seven bridges stand,
Seven churches surrounded him his folk did work the land.
In seven public houses shrewd in spending what they earn,
Seven bridges across the Calsey burn.

Born in a room on a narrow wynd,
To a family familiar with daily grind.
In Auchtermuchty fields he clambered stony walls,
An Auchtermuchty young man then recalls.
Town Band playing in the square,
Craft stalls and the market there.
Muchty made this bairn a man so grand,
In Auchtermuchty fields his folk did work the land.

From that home on a narrow wynd,
Auchtermuchty he left behind.
In Perth he met a lassie oh so fair,
He told her of the Town Band playing in Muchty Market
Square.

He asked if he'd offended, why did she bow her bonnie
head,
Distressed she seemed from what this sir had said.
Auchtermuchty childhood a kind laddie held her hand,
She answered Muchty people they are grand,
In Auchtermuchty fields, her folk did work the land.

There was a wee young lassie
In fields and Muchty market square,
Then one day the lassie was nae there.

He grew and then forgot her, so the laddie thought,
Fate once more was active and it brought.
Two bairns again united, in love about to fall,
In Auchtermuchty fields they clambered stony walls.

They came from Auchtermuchty where seven bridges stand,
Seven churches surrounded them their folk did work the
land.
In seven silent seconds love supervised that day,
Fields of Auchtermuchty may have mystified the Tay.

Auchtermuchty is in north east Fife near to the main
A91route to St Andrews. James V in the year of 1517 made
it a Royal Burgh therefore fairs and markets could be held
there. The majority of locals in the mid 1800's worked in
the linen industry and more recently whisky. The name of
Auchtermuchty came from Gaelic words meaning upland
slope of the wild pig and its flag bears a picture of a boar.
Jimmy Shand the famous accordion player lived there and
also the Scottish duo the Proclaimers. We visited there in
April 2008 and were fascinated by the narrow wynds and
buildings. My mother recalls my dad calling it 'Actamuchty'
whenever he mentioned it although I am led to believe
locals abbreviate it to 'Muchty'.

Towns and places in Fife were being added to our unwritten

list as we made our way steadily around the Kingdom. This one year I can recall first seeing the War Memorial of the Highland Infantryman in Newburgh on the north coast. Lynne and I also stopped by there on our journey with our mothers on-route to a guest house in Perth. We had stayed for two nights at the Craw's Nest Hotel in Anstruther. This would be in 2008 after I had walked my 3rd stage of the coastal path from Crail to St. Andrews.

Highland Infantryman ©

2013

Infantryman,
Highland Infantryman
more than a mile in sculpture and style
whaur ah saw ye, back in Newburgh

Can I get to Cupar?
a'for the rain come tha's due to come to Cupar,
'got to get to Cupar'

Come ye back the warm sun
that shined on me near Newburgh,
where, a Fifer joked wi' me, when he spoke wi' me
"it was God's town", obviously his town, Newburgh

Can I get to Cupar?
a'for the rain come tha's due to come to Cupar,
'got to get to Cupar'

Hedgerow grows a wild poppy
makes me think of the Infantryman,
Highland Infantryman,
and other fallen Soldiers

Gently the breeze does blow
the wild poppy on the hedgerow, near Newburgh
God bless you Soldiers

Can I get to Cupar?
a'for the rain come tha's due to come to Cupar,
'got to get to Cupar'

Gone now from, the vicinity of Newburgh
loving the lie of the land,
steadily, no time in hand

Suddenly, the rain come
a'for I got to Cupar,
ay the rain come tha's due to come to Cupar
'got to get to Cupar'

Hedgerow grows a wild poppy,
on the day I'd got to get to Cupar,
thinking of the Infantryman
Highland Infantryman,
whaur ah saw ye, back in Newburgh

where, a Fifer joked wi' me, when he spoke wi' me
"it was God's town", obviously his town, Newburgh,
God bless you Soldiers

171

Home From Home
Across The Border ©

2014

It takes me a thoughtful three hours
three hours to cross the border,
if I was to say from home
it would be hurtful, out of order.

I follow the signs for Glasgow
'dear old Glasgow town' they sing
or the rolling road to Auld Reekie
like every Queen and a King

I'm also forgetting to tell
I love the M6 Motorway oh so well
in the vicinity of the lovely Lakes
a pleasant homecoming journey it makes

Must now be getting near
for every time I come here,
my heart is strong in the beat
like a laddie and his special treat

The magnificent Forth Rail Bridge

have you ever seen the Forth Bridge?
Were your eyes admiring like mine
this creation of Victorian time

Alight is my first sight of Fife
the glorious Kingdom o' Fife,
Robert the Bruce, Dunfermline
Fife, I'm soon to be there in

I always call at K'cody
even though not knowing nobody,
near to Raith Rovers ground at K'cody
for myself and may be somebody

From K'cody o'er the rippling Forth
five hours of excitement driving north,
Auld Reekie, I see thee from near to Links Street
my heart is still strong in the beat

Kingskettle now and Collessie
Ladybank where I freely wander,
drawn to the land of my ancestry
I welcome the spell I am under

Cupar then on to St Andrews
St Andrews by the Northern Sea,

tomorrow morning to Tayport
then on to dear auld Dundee

There's a plaque on a wall in Dundee
Dundee by the silvery Tay,
William Wallace first struck a blow they say
for Scottish independence,
I read it myself there one day

Arbroath I've reason to go
Aberdeen aye I've been,
but the picturesque Northern Lights
the Aurora Borealis I have not yet seen

Does it matter how long it takes?
It takes to cross the border,
does it matter how long it takes
for self satisfaction is what it all makes

Then when it's time to go home
leaving home for home is the sense,
I love my journey to Scotland
I don't disguise or have no pretence

Reader, are you with me this far?
you've travelled yourself on foot, carriage and car,

we're now calling at Gretna Green
into England from Scotland we've been
In footsteps of many a King and Queen

On the second stage of walking the path back in 2008 I can recall stumbling on the camping and caravan site at Shell Bay. Not only was I impressed by the site but also the climb up the hills away from there and over to Earlsferry.

I've driven in there a few times since to get familiar with the site with plans of one day camping myself. I was fortunate to be able to pitch for a single night before the Easter Bank Holiday weekend in April 2011. After pitching my tent in the afternoon I was soon on my way over Kincraig to Earlsferry not only for the walk but to find a shop for some resources. I have read that this the highest point of the coastal path with the remains still there of the Battery Defences of World War 2.

Sea Tangle Road through the golf course led me into Chapel Green Road and the High Street at Earlsferry. I was struck by the peacefulness and cleanliness of the road and well-painted dwellings as I headed towards Elie.

I awoke early in my tent on Good Friday morning soon to be leisurely climbing up the hills again overlooking the bay. The mist appeared to be clinging and weather reports were requesting vehicles to reduce their speed going over the Forth Road Bridge.

Come 8.00am I was away and on route to St Andrews where I parked by the East Sands. Visibility was still poor with the castle and cathedral ruins looking eerie in the fog. My plan was to walk to the Old Course along the edge and back through the streets and return to my car to drive up to somewhere near the Tay Bridge.

From there it was a walk along the Tay for an hour or so to the ruins of Balmerino Abbey, founded in 1227 to 1229 by Cistercian monks from Melrose Abbey. It was only a couple of weeks earlier I had written 'Tell Me o'The Tay' mentioning the ruins and wanted pictures to display with the poem.

On this stretch of walk there are interesting carved seals and upon research the Dundee Courier reports that they are made by Pete Boucher from Moffat.

Good to be back on the path and good to mention that since I first starting walking the coast of Fife we are now blessed with 2 other grandchildren. A pair of lovely lassies into the fold and on to the Christmas present list.

So not am I only walking back into my roots, I am walking back into theirs, being Aaron, Liam, Kiera–Marie, Caitlyn and may be more.

Back on the Path
at Shell Bay ©

2011

Good to be back on the path
fortunate Fifeshire was gie
The lap o' the Forth
called me north
to a close proximity

Pitched a tent enriched and content
o'er Kincraig a'walking I went
a'walking o' for the view
past battery defences of World War 2

Warm the welcome and weather
up and o'er the brae
Good to be back on the path
back on the path at Shell Bay

Once more it was an early morning five hour drive to the
Kingdom of Fife. Breakfast at West Moreland another break
at Moffat and then on towards Kirkcaldy for a food shop.
My wife Lynne and I were booked into a caravan for a week
for a well deserved holiday.

It turned out to be an unsettled week but England appeared
to be having it worse with news of floods. The days here
were misty, as I soon found out when on my early morning
walk around Dairsie. I could hear the Eden flowing before I
could see it as I walked down towards Dairsie Bridge. The
River Eden I believe flows from the borders near Perth and
Kinross to the Eden Estuary into the North Sea by St
Andrews.

We had planned to attend the Cupar Highland Games on
Sunday the first day of July 2012.

The Bonnie Lassies Danced

at the

Cupar Highland Games ©

2012

Went a misty walk 'bout Dairsie

hark at the Eden

amongst the trees and bushes

hark at the Eden

under Dairsie bridge she rushes

hark at the Eden, hark at the Eden

went a July day to Cupar
hark at the pipers
coming up Bonnygate
hark at the pipers
to Duffus Park they insufflate

hark at the Pipers, hark at the Pipers

the bonnie lassies danced
at the Cupar Highland Games
don't know their names
the bonnie lassies danced
at the Cupar Highland Games

went a later browse 'bout Cupar
hark at the Eden
nearing trains, cars and buses
hark at the Eden
under South bridge she rushes

hark at the Eden, hark at the Eden

the bonnie lassies danced
at the Cupar Highland Games
don't know their names

the bonnie lassies danced
at the Cupar Highland Games

went a early drive to the west sands
hark at the ocean
down there by the dunes
hark at the ocean
playing tidal tunes

hark at the ocean, hark at the Eden,
hark at the Eden, hark at the Pipers

the bonnie lassies danced
at the Cupar Highland Games
don't know their names
the bonnie lassies danced
at the Cupar Highland Games

the bonnie lassies danced
at the Cupar Highland Games
don't know their tartan, their faces, their names
the bonnie lassies danced
at the Cupar Highland Games

went another walk 'bout Dairsie
hark at the Eden, hark at the Eden

I noticed the sign of Cupar Hearts FC on a building in 2012 whilst at the Highland Games. There was a piper practising as he must have been in the competition that was taking place. I was to later send the poem to Cupar Hearts AFC and received a complimentary reply.

The Piper Played by Cupar Hearts ©
2014

The Borders,
then Edinburgh,
'Embra', Lothian,
Embra, beyond the Borders,
Scottish Borders

South Queensferry
I gazed at what I craved,
craved, for the feeling,
in South Queensferry,
o'er the water,
from South Queensferry

Oh South Queensferry,
my journey you stall,
Forth Bridge, expansive and tall,
oh South Queensferry,
you stall my journey,
South Queensferry

K'cody,
being beside the Forth,
in K'cody,
feel my feelings rise,
in K'cody

They rise,
they rise and rise and rise,
they rise and rise and rise,
because I,
am in K'cody,

my Kennedy o' Kirkcaldy,
my K'cody

I told somebody yesterday,
I've seen Embra from K'cody,
K'cody keeps on calling,
keep on calling K'cody,
K'cody, keep on calling

The Piper played by Cupar Hearts,
he played,
The Piper played by Cupar Hearts,
and Piper's joined in and played

He played with my word,
all I've seen and heard,
heard since the Millennium,
how fortunate, this Fifers son

And when the Piper played by Cupar Hearts,
he played,
whilst his kilt, he swung and swayed,
he played.

The Piper played by Cupar Hearts,
he played, and there he made,

a heart, hurt to leave,
so there it stayed

The Borders,
past Edinburgh,
Embra, then the Borders.
Home,
beyond the Borders,
Home,
either side of the Borders

He played,
and he shan't fade,
by Cupar Hearts the Piper played

Back and forth to Fife brings many thoughts to mind with how my parents could have met. If it wasn't for the fact that they were in the British Army it would not have happened. Thinking on that journey of my parents being born so far away from each other and what one does have to do to be together. Perhaps being in the forces had prepared a move to another place upon finding a partner. The A74, at the time of writing, is only part of the many, many miles between Ladybank in Fife and Wolverhampton.

I Thought a Wee While ©

2005

While travelling back from Glasgow
Along the A74,
Hills I could see for many a mile
Their colours changed in the shadows.
I imagined, as I looked
And I thought a wee while,
How far it must have seemed
To leave a homeland and childhood behind,
And place your roots elsewhere,
I find it hard to imagine,
I find it hard to compare.

While travelling back from Glasgow
Along the A74,
The sky I could see for many a mile
And the colours still changed in the shadows.
On the hills there were buildings
Made of old stone,
I imagined, as I looked
And I thought a wee while,
How could they not want to return,
To the hills and the glens,
And the land that's inside their heart,
What was it like to keep them apart.
To me it seemed too far
As I sat there my thoughts did wonder,
While I was a traveller inside of a car.
When they never came home
Was it for somebody fair,
Is a man willing to let go of his belonging
To move on and settle elsewhere.

The evening sun shines from the west
Through the clouds there's a picturesque scene,
Twenty five miles then its England
Just beyond old Gretna Green.
All shades of grey hide the blue of the sky

I imagined, as I looked
And I thought a wee while,
'Tis soon to wish Scotland goodbye.

What I have found in my years of research is that we had a
broad range of skills and many trades. Residing by the coast
brought a living from the sea and land. I have no doubt that
I would have passed a harbour that kin of mine has sailed
from and walked by a field where they have toiled. I would
have seen the same sunrise and starry sky. Both the sun and
moon would have glistened on the Forth and Tay as I have
seen with my own eyes many times.

Fifers in our Family Tree ©
Hogmanay 2011/12

'Och for a penny in mah pooch
mah trooser pooch
in mah pooch a penny o yours
to pay my way to yesterday
and help you with your chores'

Been down mines they have down mines
in past times they have past times
Been down mines they have down mines
down mines in our ancestry

Sailed seas they have sailed seas
names and professions whatsoever be

Sailed seas they have sailed seas
Fifers in our family tree

"Och for a penny in mah pooch...

Ploughed fields they have ploughed fields
in past times they have past times
Ploughed fields they have ploughed fields
ploughed fields in our ancestry

Bridge builders they've been bridge builders
names and professions whatsoever be
Bridge builders they've been bridge builders
Fifers in our family tree

'Och for a penny in mah pooch
mah trooser pooch...

Been Labourers and Journeymen
in past times they have past times

Been Labourers and Journeymen
Journeymen in our ancestry

Been Servants they have been Maids
names and professions whatsoever be
Been Servants they have been Maids
Fifers in our family tree

'Och for a penny in mah pooch
mah trooser pooch
in mah pooch a penny o yours...

Been Coopers they have been Coopers
in past times they have past times
Been Coopers they have been Coopers
Cooper's in our ancestry

Caught fish they have caught fish
names and professions whatsoever be
Caught fish for a tasty dish
Fifers in our family tree

194

'Och for a penny in mah pooch
mah trooser pooch
in mah pooch a penny o yours
to pay my way to yesterday...

Made suits they have made shoes
in past times they have past time
Made suits they have made shoes
Shoemakers in our ancestry

Fought wars they have fought wars
names and professions whatsoever be
Fought wars for Britain's cause
Fifers in our family tree

'Och for a penny in mah pooch
mah trooser pooch
in mah pooch a penny o yours
to pay my way to yesterday
and help you with your chores'

Laid to rest to rest in France
in France where soever be
Laid to rest to rest in France
a Fifer in our ancestry
a brave Fifer in our family tree...

'Och for a penny in mah pooch
mah trooser pooch
in mah pooch a penny o yours
to pay my way to yesterday
and help you with your chores'
in mah pooch
mah well soiled trooser pooch
a King George V penny of yours!

Knowing who and what you are is a feeling and whenever I cross the border into Scotland it surfaces. Further on nearing Fife that feeling gets stronger and the crossing of the Forth Road Bridge is extra-special. There is definitely something inside of me that connects me to the Kingdom.

A Fifer Burns Inside of Me ©

2008

A Fifer burns inside of me
He unearths come now and then
Many a way he breaks my day
I cannae cage nor cannae I pen

If I build a barrier
He's bound to make an attack
The Fifer burns inside of me
He's always coming back

Like fire he burns and burns in me
Every day I dree
The Fifer keeps on burning
He keeps my mind turning
Back to Collessie and Ladybank
East Neuk places the Forth they flank
St Andrews by the shore
The Fifer burns once more

He keeps in mind the Lomond Hills
How I love that scene
The Fifer burns inside of me
He's everywhere I've been

The Fifer keeps on burning
He keeps my mind turning
Back to Collessie and Ladybank
East Neuk places the Forth they flank
St Andrews in the rain
The Fifer burns again

There are reminders of Fife spread around our home and in our hallway for many years has been a photograph taken from the height of Edinburgh Castle in 2002. It clearly shows Fife over the Forth with the lovely Lomond Hills. Along that coastline are ancestry places of mine on the Kennedy side and Bennet in central and north east of the Lomonds. That coast I have walked along and East Lomond (at the time of writing) I have climbed. The poem is also a message to my children and theirs to never forget who they are and where they came from. Whenever I look at that picture, day or night it switches on an ancestry light in my mind.

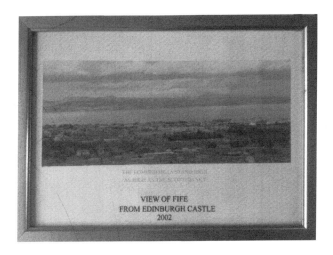

VIEW OF FIFE
FROM EDINBURGH CASTLE
2002

A Picture View ©

2009

When light is dim
Socialising I have and not long came in
A photo, a picture view
Taken way back in 2002
In our hall, not prominently
there the shores of Fife I see
Coastline and fields behind
Searching for something the back of my mind
Amazing what light and night can produce
One self can devise and deduce

Edinburgh Castle height
Over the city and water
Come ye here see what I see
Come my son and daughter

That land over there is within
Deep in your genes under your skin
In strands of your hair
Fragments of bone
Don't leave it behind
Leave it alone

Be fooled ye not by your voice
It's the Kingdom, your decision your choice
Amazing what light and night can produce
One self can devise and deduce

Over the years I began thinking more and more of Fife and St Andrews and it became my first holiday choice. We had done the popular English resort holiday with our children when young and foreign breaks on our own, but to join together time off from work and learning more about where I came from was tempting.

I can recall walking through the caravan site at Kinkell Braes and seeing the wonderful views of the East Sands and beyond. A few years later we have ourselves, at the time of writing, stayed there on three occasions, always admiring the scenery. Looking down on Shorehead and the harbour for family reasons is a favoured view of mine, and it's too far away!

You Are Too Far Away ©

2006/7

You are too far away,
I think about you every day.
Too far for me to be,
Upon your sand beside your sea.
You are too far away,
You complete my world in every way.
I recall the evening in the rain,
Your sea seemed restless but could you sustain.
I watched as the clouds masqueraded the view,
You disguised yourself as the coast wind blew.
Then your rain fell more and more,
I sat in shelter by your rocky shore.
The darkness came and night time rain,
This wretched scene you could not maintain.
No matter how you try,
I'll wait for the dark clouds to roll on by.
You will never take my feelings away,
Oh you bonnie, bonnie bay.

Oh St Andrews Bay
I love you more than words can say,
A different love that I have for my wife
A love so deep that I have for Fife

You will never take my feelings away,
Oh you bonnie, bonnie bay.
I watch the sea as I stand alone
Cover o'er the old Scottish stone
I hope someday my children see it too
The sands and the rocks and the coastal view

When they stand by the open sea,
They will think of others
Not only me.
As they gaze at the rugged coast,
A thought for those who they love most.
But what of roots and blood inside,
It's in their make-up,
It's in their pride.
One day they will understand,
Why I love your coast,
I love your land.
You will never take my feelings away,
Oh you bonnie, bonnie bay.

Oh St Andrews Bay
A rainy scene or a summer day,
Your beauty, always a joy to see
Upon your sand I love to be.
When the clouds break to heavy showers

I look out to sea and gaze for hours,
You may be dismal and rain all day
Oh you bonnie, bonnie bay

You bonnie, bonnie bay.

In time I became familiar with St Andrews and found that someone in my line worked at the Railway Station that is long since gone. The cobbled streets and water fountain gives a charming auld feeling. 'A ST ANDREWS WEDDING IN JUNE', is a fictional story poem from 1923 when trains arrived at St Andrews in a time my ancestors would have lived and known.

A ST ANDREWS
WEDDING IN JUNE ©

2013

It was in the year
of nineteen twenty three,
A laddie stepped from
the second carriage
Of a Steam train
arriving at St Andrews
Springtime flowers
were preparing to bloom

He was to fall in love
But yet, not to know
For it was too soon

His case he carried
Under the West Port
Appointment at noon
He was to fall in love
But yet, not to know
For it was too soon

His case he carried
To the Town Hall
A laddie not yet married
Along South Street nearing noon
He was to fall in love
But yet, not to know
For it was too soon

In the very same year
of nineteen twenty three
A lassie stepped from
the first carriage
Of a Steam train
arriving at St Andrews
Summer flowers were now in bloom

She was to fall in love
But yet, not to know
For it was too soon

Her case she struggled to carry
In-stepped a laddie
This laddie she was later to marry
Next summer in June
They were to fall in love
But yet, not to know
For it was too soon

Her case he carried
Along St Mary's Place
This laddie not yet married
Could not fail to notice
This lassie's pretty sweet face

They said farewell
At the dwelling where she was residing
Two weeks then passed
"Had she took to hiding? He asked

Then one Sunday
By the Major Whyte-Melville fountain

The lassie there admiring
The laddie gave up counting

"Good day" he said to her
"Hello sir" replying said she
"You're the laddie at the station"
She recalled, "kindly helping me"
It was now here on Market Street
And again nearing noon
They were to fall in love
But yet, not to know
For it was too soon

Accepting his offer
to accompany him
To see the Castle,
Cathedral ruins and St Rule's Tower
Fisher Quarter children
playing in North Street
"How swift is the hour?

Down The Pends
Along to The Scores
In St Andrews they fell in love
And here I shall pause

It was in the year
of nineteen twenty three
His heart she carried
This lassie not yet married
But coming soon
A St Andrews wedding in June

Being the son of a Fifer, It would have been great to have shared this experience or to at least him knowing that I was to be 'caught and captured' by this part of Scotland. I 'wish for this and wish for the other' and I also wish that I had been seen ancestry walking the coast when this talented Fifer was out there painting.

A Painting by Jack Vettriano ©

2009

I wish for many an obvious thing
Wealth and my health and muse what the future may bring
Thankful for all that I have but I wish I could sing

I wish I could play the piano
Strum along on a six-string guitar
Worry no more about bank balance
Own a bit of land a larger house and drive a bigger better car

Strange though I wish I were in a picture
Of a painting by Jack Vettriano
In the background walking to Largo

Rain, wind or shine
Wishful thinking of mine

Attempting for a moment or two to inscribe
Endeavour I do to describe
Wishing I had learned more in my time
At least employed avoiding prison and crime

I have the highest regard for the honest card dealt in my
hand
Admittedly I sulk and I skulk for a stretch of sand
Occasionally making me harp on and whinge
Begging his merit a royal golden fringe

Yes, I wish I were in a picture
Of a painting by Jack Vettriano
In the background walking to Largo
Rain, wind or shine
Wishful thinking of mine

Now, over ten years on from first arriving in the glorious Kingdom of Fife, I've learned plenty and and can look back in picture and mind. I trace my thoughts back to coastal villages and lovely beaches. I found that my poems kept coming and coming. I read them now and understand exactly why they had been written.

Aberdour Greets Me Kindly ©

2007

In every forward step I feel I'm walking back,
Into the land of unknown past.
I sense some kind of welcome,
Has the Kingdom accepted this man at last?

Sunshine dances upon the Forth,
My emotions are dancing too.
A magnificent day and a wonderful view.
Aberdour greets me kindly nearing mid-day,
I look back and move forward in my own way.
Accepting my existence I yearn to learn more,
Stimulating time spent by this delightful shore.
Aberdour greets me kindly didn't she so?
Aberdour she reminds me not to ever let go.

Lovely, Littoral Elie ©

2009

Let me be in Elie,

In Elie let me lay,

Let me linger in Earlsferry,

Let me loiter in the bay.

Exhilarated by Elie,

The sunny blue sky,

Elie you were lovely, Elie oh aye.

Eager to be in Earlsferry,

I nay tell a lie,

Lovely, littoral Elie, Elie oh aye.

Only a Field in Kincaple,
Only a Field in Fife ©

2006

I watch the wave of trees,
Then I turn to face the North Sea breeze.
From a resting place of a perimeter wall,
The rolling land to the sea does fall.
I stand and listen to nothing,
I listen to nothing at all.
The view I see impresses me,
Down to the Eden Estuary.

This scene does help me to unwind,
From the hustle and bustle of the daily grind.
The rolling land to the sea does fall,
I stand and listen to nothing,
I listen to nothing at all.
Only a field in Kincaple,
Only a field in Fife.
A wee short break away from the norm,
To ease the pressure of life.

In the dead of night,
I watch the lights of distant cars
Drive on out of sight.
Up the lane towards Strathkinness,
Over the brow of the hill.
In the dead of night,
It's peaceful, quiet and still.

In the early morn,
The air is fresh a new day is born.
Up the lane towards Strathkinness,
I'm on the brow of that hill.
The sky this day is cloudy grey,
The atmosphere is still.
From a resting place of a perimeter wall,
The rolling land to the sea does fall.

I stand and listen to nothing,
I listen to nothing at all.
The view I see impresses me,
Down to the Eden Estuary.
I see afar a farmer's field,
The growth of crop that it will yield.
Only a field in Kincaple,
Only a field in Fife.
A wee short break away from the norm,
To ease the pressure of life.

It was about 9.20pm on a July 2011 evening in the
departure lounge at the George Best Belfast City Airport. I
was admiring the late evening sunlight as a plane made its
way for us passengers to board the flight to Birmingham. I
was looking forward to getting home to my wife for our
early drive to Fife where we were staying at the Bay Hotel,
Pettycur.

It had been an interesting month or so as my job had once
again taken me to Canada where I had the pleasure of
seeing Niagara Falls and then to Derry - Londonderry in N.
Ireland. Since my last visit a peace bridge has been built
over the River Foyle and it was a 'must do' of mine to walk
over and back.

My colleague and I visited St Columb's Cathedral which
was in the final stages of restoration and it is an impressive
building inside and out. The Cathedral is within the walled
city in the Diocese of Derry. It was hard to believe that
within 24 hours I would be marvelling at the equally
impressive Dunfermline Abbey and the tomb of King Robert
the Bruce.

I boarded the evening flight from Belfast and found I was
seated next to a young lady who had made a day journey
for her grandmothers funeral. We were soon in

conversation talking about family and other things and before we knew it we were landing at Birmingham.

I arrived back home late that evening and found it difficult getting off to sleep. By 3.30am I gave up and decided to take the dog a walk around the fields in the dark. We set off for Scotland at 4.45am and had our breakfast break at Gretna services. Dunfermline was our next stop with a visit to the ruins and the Abbey before taking in the shops.

By mid afternoon we opened the patio doors of our hotel room to see the magnificent views over the Firth of Forth to Edinburgh. The Bay Hotel at Pettycur really is true to their word with spectacular views.

We had been warned of a wedding on the Saturday night and there may be a little noise but I am pleased to say it was not to be. There cannot be a much better view for a Bride and Groom to look out to after their wedding. As the evening light faded the lights of Edinburgh over the firth became more prominent and added to the setting. You could see tomorrow on its way to Pettycur Bay.

I had first noticed the hotel and caravan park when walking the Fife Coastal Path back in 2007. It is on the hillside over looking the Firth of Forth near to the monument where Alexander III, King of Scots 1249-1286, was killed when falling from his horse over the cliff side. Margaret, Maid of Norway, aged 3, was heir to the throne.

Early next morning I was down on the beach and around the wee harbour at Kinghorn for an hour before breakfast in the Bay Hotel and driving up to Broughty Ferry before going in to Dundee. I had other reasons to want to visit Broughty Ferry than it being a seaside place. All hands of the Lifeboat Mona were lost on the 8th December 1959 when assisting the North Carr Lightship which was reported to be adrift in St Andrews Bay. There is a song by Peggy Seeger sung by The Dubliners called The Lifeboat Mona describing the tragic event.

A total of 8 men were lost and within 2 weeks of the
disaster, remarkably 38 volunteers had put their name
forward as the new crew. Further research of mine found
that the Mona was burnt in the night as in a Viking ritual at
Cockenzie harbour on the Forth.

Another reason to want to come to Broughty Ferry as I
believe it to be the birthplace of Francis Munro as
mentioned earlier. He played for Wolves when I was a boy
and I wrote my poem called Munro o' Broughty Ferry.

We were soon in Dundee and my eyes were everywhere
looking at the street names where my ancestors have lived. I
imagined Dundee in their day and wondered what they
would have thought of the changes and that someone of
theirs would come so far to see.

It was getting late in the afternoon but I talked my wife into
us driving up to Carnoustie, where she found a golf ball
and to Arbroath where we had a famous Smokie. Arbroath
was perfect with its working harbour and lifeboat station.
As we approached Arbroath I noticed the football ground to
my right where the game against Dundee was nearing the
end.

I received a text message while in Arbroath from Gareth, my elder brother. He was planning to be at Pettycur Bay on Sunday night.

He is a character within himself and was doing the 4 points. He started his 2 week journey from Wolverhampton by arriving at Lizard Point in Cornwall the most southerly point in Britain. Then it was the journey to Lowerstoft, Suffolk the most easterly point where we were taken to many times as lads by our dad. From there he drove to Ardnamurchan, which is the mainland's most western point. He finished at Dunnet Head the most northern point where he describes birds learn to fly sideways and washing hangs horizontally on a line. Then he had the short drive home!

The interesting fact is that he drove this remarkable journey in a home made car, not a kit car he pointed out. It was based on a Triumph Herald Convertible with a body made of marine plywood and a aluminium bonnet. He had finished building it in 2000 and still retained the original registration number. It was classed as a Historic Vehicle with just a name change to ' Midge' as that is the body design name.

The caravan he was towing was built of plywood sterling
board and aluminium panels. The size was determined by
the 8 x 4 sheets. He used the chassis of a motorbike trailer
that he had built in just 2 weeks before his trip. He'd be a
rich man now if he had taken a pound off everyone who
wanted to take a photograph. I added my bit by treating
him next morning to a good Scottish breakfast in the Bay
Hotel.

On Sunday before we met my brother we visited St Monans
where again I had walked through on the Fife Coastal Path
and I was still reading books by Christopher Rush and
Willie Fyall. I felt drawn to the lovely East Neuk coastal
village to experience as near as can be first hand what they
were writing about. The church and graveyard is most
unique with it being on the lands end next to the sea.

There was a Sunday morning service ending as we were
were looking around and my wife and I were kindly invited
into the church to admire the inside of the building. It was
easy to imagine whilst in the church all those families of
earlier generations who depended on the sea for a living
praying for a safe return home of their love ones. Also the
marriages, christening and funerals of the people that
Christopher Rush and Willie Fyall have mentioned.

By lunchtime we were in St Andrews parking up on the east side at the leisure centre. The weather was brilliant and never in all my time have I seen so many people on the beaches. We spent a while, probably too long as I tested my wife's patience looking at names on grave stones. The day proved to be lucky as we soon found a name going back to the early 1800's although I needed to confirm it. After time spent in St Andrews and on the way back to the car I twisted my wife's arm to have one more look before finally going back to the hotel. It was on my mind that it may be a long time before I am able to return to St Andrews. Within minutes I had found the stone of my Gt. Gt. Grandparents who had been born and died in St Andrews.

In 2006, four years after first coming to St Andrews with my elder brother I wrote Sojourn in St Andrews, and now 2011, I felt more closer than ever. Seeing your ancestors names gives a belonging and a reason to be there. What I had achieved is answering the questions I had asked in the poem;

> *"Did they walk the same streets?*
> *Stand in the same place,*
> *Hear the waves crash,*
> *Feel the wind in their face."*

Yes they had, because I have seen the proof.

Now I was ready to go as my elder brother Gareth had sent me a text earlier telling me he had arrived at Pettycur Bay. We met up and had our picture taken with the Firth of Forth behind us before walking to Kinghorn. We turned by the War Memorial that was unveiled by Sir Ralph Anstruther in 1923 commemorating the 60 names from the First World War and 16 from the Second World War plus one from the Korean War. On an additional note since being in Kinghorn I have found that we may have an ancestral connection there by the name of Murray going back to at least the late 1700's but that has to be confirmed. We had a couple of pints in the Carousel to celebrate our meeting in Fife and Gareth's 4 point achievements.

Before breakfast Gareth and I had an early morning walk down to the sands at Kinghorn, He admired an old Austin A 40 Devon that was parked up and we presumed it to be a lobster fisherman's who was out there in the firth. We also noticed it again as we were speaking about it driving towards Burntisland while we were having breakfast. I also took a photo on my mobile phone of a thistle that was growing near the quayside wall. Seeing the thistle in Scotland at that moment seemed perfect timing.

Next morning as my wife and I were about to drive out of the Bay Hotel, Pettycur I called to a bloke from Glasgow who was on the site talking to my brother the night before. "Has he gone yet?. "Aye" he replied, "went about half hour ago". His plans were to head for Edinburgh for a few days and if someone had seen him along the way they were sure to notice him.

The Morra Was On The Way to Pettycur Bay ©

2011

Love, a laddie, he fell,
with his lassie he fell in love
in love with his lassie he fell

Love her figure, love her face
love, a feeling for a person, a place
love, he feels it now
as the morra was on the way,
coming to Pettycur Bay.

All you grooms and beautiful brides
bonnie little bridesmaids
playing outside
as the morra was on the way,
coming to Pettycur Bay.

Love her lips, love her eyes
love is alive as the daylight dies
the morra was on the way,
coming to Pettycur Bay.

Love, a laddie, he fell,
with his lassie he fell in love
in love with his lassie he fell

Love, a laddie, he fell,
with the east coast Caledonia as well
as the morra was on the way,
coming to Pettycur Bay.

It was hard to believe the time that has passed since first researching deeper into our Scottish roots. Although putting it in the written word, I have always wondered if family members of the next generation would follow and see it for themselves.

In 2009 I had wrote 'Kingdom Come', a poem of whether or not a grandchild of mine will ever set foot in Fife.

Kingdom Come ©
2009

If a Grandchild crosses o'er the Forth
shall I weep?
With a happy heart shall I sleep?

Gracious because they have looked beyond the obvious
gone o'er the daily horizon,
delve they must and have to go far
to discover themselves and who they are.

Will they have the thirst for kindred research
walk in the shadow of Collessie church,
intent to conjoin in Kingskettle.

Back to the Kingdom they came
experience the feeling of reading a name,
who, what and where, I prepare for the question
engaging themselves in ancestry digestion.

If a Grandchild crosses o'er the Forth
shall I cry?
Will it happen before I die?

Content, satisfied, sad and proud too
If a Grandchild crosses o'er the Forth
signifying my wish has come true.

It was a cloudy Good Friday morning 2012 when 3 generations of Bennett's drove over the Forth heading first for Collessie and then Ladybank. We had our picture taken at the War Memorial where I am in possession of a newspaper cutting reporting that 'Mr H. Bennet, Picture House Manager had allowed it to be used for raising funds for the War Memorial'. I should imagine that it would be after the First World War as he had passed away himself before the Second.

After lunch in the Ladybank Tavern, as my wife and I often do, we then made tracks for Kingskettle and then onto Pettycur Bay where we had booked a long weekend in a caravan. The weather was mixed throughout as I pointed to signs of rain at Edinburgh across the Forth.

Next day was spent around St Andrews, parking near the East Sands. It was touching to see family of mine playing where ancestors before them would have been. Sailing back and forth on fisher boats, Baker's, Domestic Servants, Railway Porter's and grafting in the now demolished Gas Works.

Over the years I had found addresses, gravestones and a name on the War Memorial in St Andrews and it was a proud feeling to show them to other descendants.

On the evening, back on the south coast, we had booked a table in the Burntisland Sands Hotel. I had visited there earlier to ask if they were 'child friendly? "Extremely" I was told. I had asked as we had 2 children in our party aged 5 and under. "And we have rabbits out the back for them to take a wee look at" she said in a welcome manner. Staff were helpful with a child seat for the youngest and soon on the scene when the evening sun was in her eyes, kindly drawing the curtains. 'Friendly Fifers' I thought, recalling a poem I had wrote in 2007 about being here in Burntisland.

After our meal before strolling along the sands, I wanted to show them the Beach House where I had stayed in 2007 when first walking the Fife Coastal Path. They were taken by the park and expressed an interest to come back there the next day for the children to play. It proved to be a chilly but pleasant setting with the church bells chiming and trains occasionally passing by.

I had pointed out the monument on the road to Pettycur where Alexander III had fallen over the cliff. For the next couple of days, whenever we passed by I asked my grandson "what happened there? He excitedly answered "the King fell off his horse!"

The next evening we once again booked a meal in the Burntisland Sands Hotel as they were true to their word 'extremely child friendly' and their meals and service were very good. Highly recommended by the Bennett's and a credit to Burntisland and the Kingdom of Fife.

Although it proved to be a long Bank Holiday journey back, I had driven a child of mine and family o'er the Forth and could tell that they had connected wholeheartedly with Fife. I have the feeling that in time others will follow.

Joy of families being around a fire in the 'auld' days and reciting stories and prayers. "Lang may yer lum reek" is a Scottish salutation meaning long may your chimney smoke, long life, prosperity and your house be homely and warm. Accordingly this was a saying of Dad's but he added, "and may you always burn someone else's coal"

My Ancestors They ©

2012

My ancestors they
whether about,
down the road or o'er the border
or much further awa'

reciting stories by the fireside
in a room with a flame
that flickers awa'
and lights up all the grey
evening smokes the lum

surely be shadows
and surely be eyes
that say goodnight, hello, goodbyes
evening smokes the lum

that says day's done
work's o'er they know
and in their eyes
reflects the fireside glow
evening smokes the lum

surely those walls
surely those shadows will fade and fall
and surely those eyes that you love so
shall say God bless
in that fireside glow
evening smokes the lum

and surely those eyes that you love so
shall say next morning
with eyes of good morning hello

My ancestors they
whether about,
down the road or o'er the border
or much further awa'

told stories of the roadside
the hillside, the loch side, the seaside,
the riverside and Shropshire Union Canal side,

237

and aside the Forth and Tay
My ancestors they

My ancestors anywhere
recite the Lords Prayer
My ancestors they

Kirk an' church on the Sabbath
in best attire
festive season around a table
stories by the fire
a Scottish Wulfrunian fire
evening smokes the lum

surely be shadows
and surely be eyes
that closed, then tears
in my ancestors years

My ancestors anywhere
recited they did the Lords Prayer.
Pater Noster, Our Father
let them prey
My ancestors they

My ancestors everywhere
prayed for us all
in their prayer.....

winter snow, melting sun
evening smoked the lum...

It has been just over a decade since I found St Andrews, or did St Andrews find me? A wee bit like, finding a love your heart will call, as I wrote in my poem "The Bonnie, Bonnie Sands of St Andrews Bay, if you stand and admire you will finally fall"..

Since then I keep on returning like a pilgrim in olden days. St Andrews really does something to you, simply because it is beautiful, and long let it remain so. I have thought about it many times, is it the sea, sand, town itself, the locality? I loved the look of the buildings, the views when approaching by road, maybe but more than that, when walking the coastal path.

So what have I found in that time? Birth's, death's, addresses and names on war memorials. So to repeat myself, who found who?

The second weekend in May was approaching and we were preparing for our first visit of the year to Scotland. We made our usual early start, breakfast at West Moreland Services, up through the Borders towards Glasgow and east to Edinburgh and the Forth Bridge.

Fife looked welcoming in the morning sunshine as what was a mixed weather forecast. The first port of call was

Abbotshall Church in Kirkcaldy. I had in the past few months found that on a memorial inside the church is the name of a Kirkcaldy soldier who rests in peace in France, he died of injuries in 1917. This brave soldier I believe is in my direct line. Two attempts to find the church or hall open failed. It was rather disappointing as when peeping through a wee window by the entrance I could see the plaque.

We parked up on the seafront at Kirkcaldy with our shopping resources for the weekend and ate our lunch on a bench in Links Street. Sadly times are changing as there appeared to be empty shops in interesting buildings crying out to be loved. Another High Street made to suffer for the out of town stores I wonder?

I have always admired the mile long seafront of Kirkcaldy that has magnificent views. It has gave me many a well earned recovery hour after a long drive. When you live too far away from the coast to see it on a daily basis, do those who can, appreciate and see the natural beauty or is taken for granted, I asked myself?

A short stop at Kingskettle and Ladybank then on to St Andrews and our caravan at Kinkell Braes. We arrived about 3.00pm to a warm welcome and were given the keys for A14 with stunning views of the East Sands and beyond.

After settling in we had a tea time drink in the clubhouse about 100 yards away from the caravan door. Bar Manager Scott and all staff on site that we met were very friendly.

Earlier in the day I had spoken on the phone to Liam, our second eldest grandson and Kiera-Marie's elder brother. "Grandad, are you in Scotland yet?" he asked. "Yes I replied". "Wow", he said, and was gone before I could say anything else.

I awoke early to the sound of rain on the caravan roof. Outside the rabbits were scurrying about as I walked down the hill towards the East Sands. Along the coastal path were benches with names of those who had enjoyed St Andrews long before my discovery of her natural beauty. I made my way to the far end of the harbour wall where the wind was brisk and chill, a real Scottish wake up call.

Looking back to Shorehead I could not help but imagine my great grandmother in her childhood playing on the sands where in recent years they run on into the sea at dawn on the 1st May. This special day in the yearly calender is the birthday of Caitlyn our grandaughter. She was here last year being pushed along the path in her buggy. Our son Steven and grandson Aaron were at first sitting side by side on the wall looking at the sea and walking on the sands.

242

After breakfast next morning we drove over the Tay Bridge at Dundee. I quite like the short journey between St Andrews and Dundee, the journey that my ancestor's would have made generations ago. With Dundee growing with industry and as a means to earn a living. We were heading for Monikie, a village in Angus north east of Dundee.

We stopped at Monikie Memorial Hall, slightly raised on a corner with a good view east to the North Sea. It was camera time. I had noticed that there was a 10k run the following day at Monikie County Park and the old me would have lapped it up but the me of the day thought different!

We wondered about the grounds of Monikie Parish Church, built in 1812 on the edge of farmland in peacefulness rural surroundings. It all seemed a million miles away from our normal way of life but accordingly a certain Bennet was christened and married here in the late 1700's. More proof is needed to be sure of that genealogy theory and is questionable. The earlier generation led us further west to Inverarity. I couldn't help but look at kirk doors and wonder if anyone I descend from had walked in and out of them? The views would not have changed much, only the trees being more mature.

We were soon heading north east to the coastal resort town of Montrose where we parked by the statue of Bamse, the popular dog hero. Montrose has a deep feel of the sea trading industry and because of William Lamb ARSA is known of the sculpture capital of Angus with 23 statues scattered around. We visited the RNLI Shop that had only opened the weekend before, although small, a nice conversation we were to have with delightful staff. Soon because of the chilling wind down by the sands we were back on the road to Arbroath, another ancestral place in the 1700's if research is correct.

Whether or not I had driven and trod the exact land of where we once were or still are? There was certainly a draw in olden times to Dundee with the shipping industry, jute weaving, trading and immigration.

Returning to our caravan in St Andrews, our 'home' for the weekend at the other side of the Tay, I could see the East Sands and ruins from the caravan window. It's been 5 years since this great grandson had 'walked ower the brae', and I looked further north to the hills beyond Dundee to Angus, the birthplace of Scotland, and wondered where will I go next?

Another ancestral led time, on the right or wrong path, but closer to the folk of the east coast of Scotland, wondering who walked down this lane, out of that door, toiled in that field, a far away Scottish field?

Far Away Scottish Fields ©

2013

I've been further than,
beyond my wildest dreams
Drawn, sometimes it seems
Ne'er did I plan, to go to this extreme
Near this field of green,
beyond my wildest dream

Unearthing soil, ancient soil, shifting weeds

245

Sieving and sifting like flour,
following leads, planting new seeds
There I shall harvest all I've sown
The wee bit o crop I've grown
From Scottish fields
Far away Scottish fields

Wee bit o crop o history
Wee bit o crop o mystery
Wee bit o crop o yore
Wee bit o crop o present,
tomorrow and more

I've been further than, much further than,
beyond my wildest dreams
Ploughing whatever the land doth shield
Laden with what I yield
From Scottish fields
Far away Scottish fields

246

On the 19th June 2013 came the announcement that Wolves were to play East Fife at Bayview in a pre-season friendly. Good news for me with an ancestral interest in both Wolverhampton and Fife.

Those who have read earlier writing of mine may recall Fifer's Day. This is an ode of mine about East Fife winning the Scottish Cup in 1938. The Fifer's became the only Second Division team to win Scotland's greatest trophy.

This all came about with me calling into the football club whilst walking the Fife Coastal Path. I was made extremely welcome at Bayview and ever since then I often take a look at the ground when in Fife and always look out for their result. Last year my son, grandson and myself had our photograph taken outside the ground by their mini-bus.

I made my decision to have to be there for the game and started to plan ahead. I first called East Fife Football Club to see if it was all ticket or could I pay on the gate. Upon speaking to a most pleasant gentleman named Denis, he could tell from my accent that I was not a local but from the Midlands. I told him my name and explained to him my interest in Fife and to my surprise he was not only aware of my ode Fifer's Day, he also had it on his computer!

Fifers Day 1938 ©

2007

A dressing room team talk on cup final day,
'Believe in yourselves and show you can play'.
'We all have a chance how small or how great',
But to win or to lose could be fate?

From the very first whistle their defence stayed strong,
But it had to be asked for how long.
A division two team were under attack,
A relentless opponent kept pushing them back.
Killie snarled and roared,
Then McKerrell the Fifer unleashed a great strike,
The minnows from Methil had scored.
I read that the tide then turned for Killie,
Twice the Fifers were forced to concede.
Odds on favourites were Killie,
On course at half time with a two one lead.

The teams then returned to commence,
Surely not an upset could a Killie fan sense.
For the next ten minutes the men from Fife,
Hung on to their footballing life.
Then on the hour came the Fifers reply,
Killie were behind when McLeod twisted high.

His acrobatic goal that day was a gem,
They nae lost the lead again.

Extra time beckoned for the two weary teams,
The Scottish Cup Final and football dreams.
A bosses team talk is believe what I say,
'This is to be an underdog day'.
Black and gold coloured supporters then roared,
Miller for the Fifers had scored.

Killie then faded with the afternoon light.
Their dream of this trophy was soon out of sight.
In 1938 came a memorable day,
Over 91,000 watched this final replay.
When McKerrell scored goal number four,
He sent many a Killie to the exit door.
This game now became well beyond doubt,
The gold and black colours once again came out.
East Fife 4 Kilmarnock 2,
The trophy that year went to Bayview.

Time now to think ahead about where to stay for the night and the decision was to take my tent. A couple of years earlier on Good Friday 2010, I had camped at Shell Bay, now Elie Holiday Park. It really is a delightful site and once again I had came across it whilst walking the Fife Coastal Path. All done, there was to be a pitch awaiting for me for the evening of Wednesday 10th July.

My plan was to set out from my Codsall home as early as possible so I could get a day's walking in before going to the game on the evening. Next day was also to be an early start to set off to home as unfortunately my uncle Eddy Owen had passed away aged 89years and his funeral was early Thursday afternoon. He had also been a footballing man and whenever we were to meet he would call "get the ball out!"

At 3.41am on Wednesday morning I set off from my Codsall home and crossed the border at about 6.20am. It was perfect driving weather but the weather was predicting a cloudier day north and west. The Forth Bridge at South Queensferry was my planned stop and I arrived at 8.30am, changed into my walking shoes and made my way to walk over the Forth Road Bridge.

It was really breezy upon the bridge and I had read and found it to be correct that you can feel the vibration of the traffic through the steelwork.

The Forth Road Bridge opened in 1964 and there has been a main crossing of the Forth at South Queensferry by means of ferry since at least 1071. Malcolm III for the Queen, Saint Margaret of Scotland, allowed free passage there mostly for pilgrims heading for St Andrews. The Forth Road Bridge is one and a half miles long and when first built was the longest in Europe. There's soon to be another crossing built further west along the Forth.

I once wrote of a young man of aged 16 who lost his life whilst employed building the rail bridge. Thomas Joseph Harris's name is on the new monument's both sides of the Forth naming the unfortunate men who lost their lives.

It makes it all seem so real and sad when you read names of men who lost their lives building the bridge. I for one have the same emotions when crossing the Forth and can only imagine the challenges those men endured.

Once over the road bridge I made my way to North
Queensferry. The clouds were low over the cantilever's of
the rail bridge but the weather forecast was promising for
the afternoon. At the war memorial I engaged myself into
conversation with a gentleman who was happily whistling
away. I asked him the route to the station and he pointed
and said "that way, up cardiac hill, there is an handrail if
you're struggling". I caught the 10.42am to Dalmeny and
have now been over the Forth Bridge on a train!

Abbotshall Parish Church in Kirkcaldy was my next destination to once again try to get a photograph of a memorial plaque. The reason being that there is a certain Kennedy that I believe to descend from who is named. Three times I had been unsuccessful in May as the church was locked. This time I had a stroke of luck as I arrived at the same time as a gentleman who had keys!

Abbotshall Parish Church, Kirkcaldy.

Andrew Duncan kindly allowed me to take a photo and even better sent to me his picture taken from his camera. Andrew was to also send a very nice complimentary e-mail.

255

"Hi Robbie,

Please, by all means, use the photo as you wish. I will be
very proud to see it on your site.
I have already directed a couple of fitba' daft friends to your
site and Abbotshall's minister, Rosie Frew (for the poetry).
Take care,
Andrew Duncan"

SOLDIER, KIRKCALDY SOLDIER ©

2012

Soldier,
Kirkcaldy Soldier
how you fought your way through France
for freedoms fight, the chance
increase the right for peace
to live in peace
Soldier,
Kirkcaldy Soldier

ne'er did you come home
or grow older
Soldier,
Kirkcaldy Soldier

there builds sadness, an inner tear
your bravery, your fear
you Lancashire Fusilier
dearest Soldier
Kirkcaldy Soldier

your name, your stone
from the Great War
and on the Church wall at Abbotshall
proud of you Soldier
Kirkcaldy Soldier

years have passed
were winters colder?
those muddy trenches
Soldier,
Kirkcaldy Soldier
in fields you fought in France
for freedoms fight, the chance
increase the right for peace
rest in peace
courageous Soldier
Kirkcaldy Soldier

Shell Bay was next to pitch my tent and a stroll to the shore before heading to Leven. Once by the shore the peacefulness struck me and then I was over powered by the feelings I had when walking the Fife Coastal Path back in 2007.

An afternoon of walking down at Leven and it was strange to see the towers not standing overlooking Bayview. Down on the front I got talking to a gentleman by the name of Bill Meddings from Rugeley who was here for the game and is a devoted home and away Wolves supporter.

It was a good evening for a pre-season friendly and the lady on the Fifer's loudspeaker was amusing with her pronouncement of names. The crowd were laughing almost every time and she was aware. As the game was drawing to a close she announced a smashing good luck message to Wolverhampton Wanderers FC from East Fife FC for the new season. I once wrote of a 'Friendly Fifer said Hello' and here was a friendly Fifer saying 'Cheerio!

5.00am start in the morning for home for my Uncle Eddy's funeral in early afternoon. "Get the ball out Robbie", he used to say when seeing me. It surely was Uncle Eddy!

He was a bit of an artist, maybe he made me see the colours of that rainbow just as I entered Bayview?

In the year 1903, our Bennet travelled o'er The Tay from Dundee to Fife, residing in Tayport (Ferryport-on-Craig). In 2013, another man named Bennett, came a travelling that way!

(Note one T and two T's in Bennet(t) but still the same line).

It has been since around the year of 2000 that I have been wandering about Fife and Dundee, the home of my Scottish ancestry. The early start or an overnight drive from my home in Codsall, Staffordshire to see the dawning of day on the east coast of Scotland.

Since doing so there has been interest in my writing with requests to being a featured poet on certain websites in Scotland.

Many times I have visited Tayport and gazed across the mighty Tay to Dundee and Broughty Ferry. I have always noticed the Bell Rock Tavern and fancied calling in for a pint but never had until summer of 2013.

In 2008 when walking the Fife Coastal Path from St Andrews to Dundee, I was to rest on the wall there to grease my blistered feet before carrying on along Dalgleish Street. In the year 1903, as mentioned, our Bennet travelled o'er The Tay from Dundee to Fife and lived here. Branches from that family went to England, United States of America, Canada and one I believe who was born there to Australia.

Accordingly The Bell Rock Tavern has been there since 1887 therefore one hour of our time in 2013 on the terrace with drink in hand, brought ancestral feelings.

I was as 'proud as punch' for the Bennet family last night to find that my poem, The Terrace of The Bell Rock Tavern, is on their History Page.

THE TERRACE of
THE BELL ROCK TAVERN ©

2013

Had a great day
In Dundee o'er The Tay
This man named Bennett
Went a travelling that way
To Dundee o'er The Tay

And don't she look fine?
Every Dundonian of mine
In bygone time

Dundonian's o mine
Let me rhyme, Dundee looks fine

Drawing me there
Seagate, Murraygate,
Everywhere we did walk
Listening to Dundonian's talk

To top a great day
In Tayport back o'er The Tay
Upon the terrace of
The Bell Rock Tavern
Looking out o'er The Tay

The Bell Rock Tavern
On Dalgleish Street
Hospitality great, a welcome greet
In Tayport o'er The Tay
Where a hundred years a' more
A man named Bennet came a travelling that way
To Tayport o'er The Tay

But today is today
In The Bell Rock Tavern
A man named Bennett
Who would have thought it today?

263

Climbing steps, up and down and each way
Looking o'er The Mighty Tay

From The Bell Rock Tavern
Wrestling I am with past time
Those old Dundonian's of mine
Playing on my mind

A man named Bennett
Whose bound to have the last say
That terrace on The Bell Rock Tavern
Topped a great day
So call in yourself one day!

My wife Lynne and myself more so because of the many times she has accompanied me were getting familiar with the roads and towns of Fife. It has grown into our second home and at times I have to remind myself that we are really there. We have pictures and memories from a decade and more of holidays here.

I can recall approaching a traffic island not far from the Forth Bridge in 2007 with the feeling of starting my stretch of the coastal path. Also seeing the Saltire Flag flying from the Beach House in Burntisland when searching for my home for a couple of days.

The buildings, roads, hills, sea and views, knowing what may be around the corner. I was learning plenty and wanted more. A description of me from May at Scotland's Enchanted Kingdom, "I think that you can really call yourself a Scot, Robbie! In fact you are almost a real Fifer.

She has in the past been most complimentary of my writing and in 2008 she wrote of my poem Sojourn in St Andrews;

"Robbie, not only have you described some of the highlights of St Andrews (one of my many favourite places in the world) -but the Scottish blood in you runs deep. You may live in England; and for all I know have an English accent, but your love for Scotland and for Fife really shines through. There's no doubt you are a Scot at heart."

Fife My Friend ©

2009

Fife my friend do you remember me
or do I display too much familiarity?
I crave your very place on earth
merely a man of word and little worth
I am drawn dear Fife, you are inbred and worn
I am torn dear Fife, I am torn.
Fife my friend say you remember me
I warm to you as family
you always raise my spirit, the moment I arrive
Fife, the simple reason I'm alive.

This Public Bar in Ladybank ©

2006

Old pictures of a local scene,
Where they may have passed by or may have been,
On this day, I'm pleased to say,
I walked into a bar in Ladybank.

Ladybank Tavern I had found
Where my roots and relations were once around,
I saw this pub, by the railway line in Ladybank.

What would the old folk have thought
if they could see me here?
In this place politely ordering
a pint and a half of Tennents beer.

She told me it was the Railway Tavern
For many years before,
Then I heard some local voices talking,
As they came in through the roadside door.

In Ladybank Tavern my imagination then made me see,
In the company of relations passed,
They all surrounded me.
Some had seen two wars and more,
Am I local as voices by the roadside door?
In a public bar, by the railway line in Ladybank.

In Ladybank Tavern in the month of May,
I drank a beer for all that day.
But they have all passed on and gone,
So I drink my pint and travel on.
But on this day, I'm pleased to say,
I was in Ladybank.

Thinking of my Dad's childhood days while I was in Ladybank and wishing he were here with me. Looking at things he would have seen and wondering what changes have been made since he went away to join the army. While I was on the station platform the train to Dundee approached. I watched as it departed Ladybank gradually turning to the east and out of sight. I imagined my Dad doing the same but listening to the engine building up the power and watching the steam that would have be seen for many a mile.

Regarding the War Memorial where I have mentioned 'we'll read every soldiers name.' I am in possession of a paper cutting about Ladybank sent to me from a relative living in Louisiana. It reports that manager Mr H. Bennet gave over the Picture House for 2 evenings to raise money for the War Memorial fund. (Hector Bennet was my Great Grandfather and lived in Monkstown). Within the entertainment were artistic dances by Miss Lizzie Reid of Church Street and special films from Provost Crichton. Quote from that report, 'The accommodation was taxed to its utmost, and the drawings amounted to £23.' Unfortunately I do not know what year this would have been.

Upon researching more about the Ladybank War Memorial in September 2011, the Architect George Charles Campbell 1882 – 1932 may have been involved in the project from after the year of 1918.

Come Stand With Me
In Ladybank ©

2009

He would have told me,
Here's Monkstown, where I lived Robbie.
If only, he had told me,
There's his home, that's where he lived.

He would have told me,
Steam trains were plenty in Ladybank.
If only, he had told me,
Stories of old in Ladybank.

I never thought to question him,
I was pre-occupied.
I lost my opportunity,
I wish I had before he died.

On the platform alone in Ladybank,
The Dundee train commutes on through.
If only, he had told me,
The train to Dundee he's seen it too.

272

Come see the Lomonds from Ladybank,
Come wait at the station and stand with me.
We'll stand together,
We'll call in at Cupar and dine in Dundee.

Let's wear a poppy in Ladybank,
We've worn one we have elsewhere.
He never told me,
I'm pleased you've been,
I'm glad you're there.

Come stand with me in Ladybank,
We'll read every soldiers name.
He never told me,
I'm pleased you've been,
I'm glad you came.

A reminding poem for my children and theirs of family history. It is very easy in modern day comforts to not understand our past. Our forefathers may have had to give up their homes and even sailed to far foreign shores for a brighter future. Our direct line was meeting whilst in the British Army.

Never Cheer Against Scotland ©

2010

Think like English you may
Be English by birth you be
Never cheer against Scotland
Bonnie Scotland is inside of ye

There may come a time up and creep
A cheap and insulting remark
It shall cut through to a sensitive feeling
a stab it shall be in the dark

Think like English you may
Be English by birth you be

Never cheer against Scotland
For Scottish is inside of ye

Parent, Grandfather, Great Grandparents,
Fife and onto Dundee
Never cheer against Scotland
For Scotland is one side of ye

Caledonia will need your defence
You will feel it, you'll know it, you'll see
Never cheer against Scotland
against Scotland, for the auld enemy

Scotland didnae Die ©

2009

Love and adore
I want to see you more,
I wear your flower
and I wait for the hour
that I return to Scotland

My heart does burn
sets me on fire,
with passionate desire

Hampden and Murrayfield,
my heart did burn with pride
a son was there for you
you didnae know that he didnae hide

Wearing your flower
most days and hour
your flower,
the national emblem of Scotland

No need to question
or ask me why,
for when you sadly passed away
Scotland didnae die

It's What You Are ©

2006

Greater than where you were born
It's what you are that counts,
As you live your life
Distinction builds and amounts.

Whatever you are is set in your ways,
To live and grow within your days.
Surface at will come now and again,
Inside of your genes it will always remain.

Generations preceding have gave you your looks,
Your kinfolk are written in genealogy books.
It's not in your accent whenever you talk,
It's how your bones grow and the way that you walk.

Not colour of skin or land of birth,
You're placed without choice on some part of earth.
Whatever your start in your mind, body and heart,
Distinction builds and amounts,
It's what you are that counts.

It's quite simple really, there is more to a person than where they were born. We are born with characteristics that our kinfolk have given and upon gaining adulthood you may or may not choose to want to find out more. A person can actually experience a belonging feeling when in a land of their ancestors.

Examples from those who have experienced that feeling;

In 1968 Neil Armstrong, the first man to step foot on the moon, took with him a piece of tartan. Armstrong's ancestors were actually Border Scots and tartan was seen as Highland dress. Nevertheless he chose to take a piece of tartan with him for his heritage and a symbol of Scotland.

Neil Armstrong later visited Langholm for the first time in the Lowlands of Scotland. He described a 'strong feeling of home' when first arriving that he had never experienced before. This sensation was even stronger than setting foot on the moon. He admitted that it was a feeling like having an affair because he had found love elsewhere.

I can understand Neil Armstrong feelings as there is a line in my Sojourn in St Andrews, "in thought I cross the family divide".

Quote from the author of McCarthy's Bar, the late Peter McCarthy, after writing his story about finding his roots:

"I told someone during a drinking session that 'I don't feel English, even though I was born and grew up in Warrington', but I still felt the same the next day when I was sober. I may speak with an English accent but I feel Irish inside, and it's what you feel that counts".

Above are two people who have made the decision to trace their family history. Little did they know it would change the outlook on their life. Never before has it been more popular to do so with the help of the internet and television programmes researching for celebrities. To actually return to the land of your ancestors enhances a persons belonging. It is common for a person to have stronger sense of a loyalty divide towards what is further away.

It is also possible for someone to have strong feelings for their roots. They don't become less of a citizen of the land of their birth, they become more cosmopolitan. Unless you go, you'll never know.

Going about Fife and visiting places that mean something to me because of my Scottish ancestry, not knowing that there was a couple of Wolverhampton Owen's on the Old Course, even posing for a photo on the Swilcan Bridge! This means that there were more Wulfrunian Footprints in Fife other than mine!

Thinking o' Fife an' Dundee ©

2010

Just once, maybe once,
I'll tek time for a pint in the Lomond Tavern,
and the sea of thought will deliver,
a wee wave of something tae be thinking about.

And a betting man will bet,
and a winning man will get,
his winnings if he bet
that this fella' was thinking o' Fife.

Fife are ye thinking o' me?

Thinking o' Fife an o' Falkland,
and get to the top o' East Lomond,
quiet for heavens sake,
early hour, for those not awake.

Just once, another once,
I'll tek time for a pint in Ladybank Tavern,
And the sea of thought will push, push and shove,
Fife, yer fit me like a protective glove.

282

And a betting man will bet,
and a winning man will get,
his winnings if he bet
that this fella' was thinking o' Fife.

Fife are ye thinking o' me?

Thinking o' Fife an o' Saunt Aundraes
on the Old Course Golfers will be
excited to be in Saunt Aundraes
Paul and Joey O teeing off by the sea

Just once, maybe once,
I'll tek time for a pint in the Bell Rock Tavern,
and the sea of thought will deliver,
a wee wave of something tae be thinking about.

And a betting man will bet,
and a winning man will get,
his winnings if he bet
that this fella' was thinking o' Fife.

Fife are ye thinking o' me?

Thinking o' Fife an o' Tayport
Fife, where I lang to be
time to cross o'er the Tay to Angus
time to think o' Dundee

Dundee are ye thinking o' me?

Another 'I wish I would have done it different ode'. St Andrews United JFC a North East Fife Football Club who in 1960 won the Scottish Junior Cup Final on Hampden Park.

In August of 2013 I had the pleasure of attending the Tayport FC v St Andrews United fixture. It was a lively game on a pleasant summer evening up near the shores of the Tay.

I would have liked to have purchased a programme for keepsake but being as it was a midweek game there was not any on sale. Nevertheless the teams for the game that evening were displayed near the entrance.

I drove back to St Andrews after the game between two ancestral homes as a grand summer evening was drawing in. I found that I was thinking of my own footballing days and wishing that I was 40 years younger.

'Oh the game of football, leads you a merry dance'.

RUN ON WITH
ST ANDREWS UNITED ©

2013

If I could get my boots on
get my boots on
If I could get my boots back on
I'd get them on and run on
with St Andrews United

Run on to Recreation Park
with the east coast Saints
before my days come dark
2013 and on

If I could get my boots on
where have all my boots gone?
If I could get my boots back on

286

I'd get them on and run on
with St Andrews United

Run on to Hampden Park
with the east coast Saints
before my days come dark
1960 dream on

If I could get my boots on
where's 'my' 1960's boots gone?
my sharp shooting boots back on
I'd get them on and run on
with St Andrews United

Accordingly, there's mighty proud history
in the medieval town of St Andrews
there's been men putting boots on
Putting old fashioned boots on
since 1893

Makes me want to get my boots on
my 70's, 80's boots on
If I could get my 90's boots back on
I'd get them on and run on
with St Andrews United

I'd put them on for people
put them on for names
Put them on for St Andrews
in league or cup fixture games

'Cause whenever I'm in St Andrews
nearing Recreation Park
I take a wee glimpse at the lush green grass
too young I was for Hampden Park

And too old to get my boots on
get my boots on
Too old to get my boots back on
to run on for the late old man
run on with St Andrews United

Run on to Recreation Park
with the east coast Saints
Before my days come dark
for my dad and my roots
but I've got nae boots!

It was a foggy morning at just past 5.00am on Thursday 24th April 2014 when we set off from Codsall heading for Fife and Angus. This my 60th birthday trip mixed with Homecoming Scotland 2014. Eventually the fog lifted when we were beyond Manchester and nearing the Lake District. After a leisurely 3 hour drive we crossed the border at 8.05am, rested and had breakfast at Gretna Services.

Sun is shining, birds are singing, the Lomonds look magnificent, as I write these couple of lines aside the gravestone of my gt grandparents in Kingskettle. I cannot ever recall in this lifetime of mine being in such a peaceful setting.

From there we stopped by at Ladybank as I wanted to take a new photo of the War Memorial that Hector Bennet played his part in fund raising for. As mentioned earlier he was the Picture House manager at the time and let-out the building.

Time now to head for our guest house for the evening on the other side of the Tay at Broughty Ferry.

It was a grey overcast Friday morning at 5.15am as I stepped out of the Abertay Guest House on the Monifieth Road in Broughty Ferry. My plan was to catch an early bus into Dundee. It was there at Seagate Bus Station that I had finished my Fife Coastal Path walk in 2008 and where I wanted to extend that walk to Broughty Ferry. Wulfrunian Footsteps were now striding out into Angus.

I sat on the bus with half a dozen locals who I should imagine were on the way to their various employment. 'Your next stop is Seagate' came up on the screen, it certainly was, over a hundred years later than kin of mine.

I disembarked the bus at 6.00am to take a couple of photos of the Seagate area, where my Bennet's once resided. Soon I was on my way to spend a wee while around the docks. Accordingly John Bennet who I descend from was a machine fitter in the shipping industry. There beside the Tay I stayed awhile and admired the Road Bridge where I could see vehicles drive in and out of the sea mist over on the Fife side.

I made my way back from the docks to walk along the main road from Dundee with traffic and trains either side of me. It was about half way of the 5 mile walk that I was able to get down beside the Tay and stroll towards Broughty. It was still a grey sky and the drizzle of rain impeded my sight as it clung to my glasses. In the mist I could make out the castle at Broughty Ferry where my walk was to end. Short but sweet but what I had wanted to do for a year or more.

My wife was waiting for me back near the guest house on Monifieth Road and claims that she could tell it was me from a long way away. I wonder how?

Afterwards it was shopping around Dundee, the 'toast for Hector' in The Town House pub and to our caravan that awaited us in St Andrews. It was raining and became really heavy overnight and as always appears worse when in a caravan.

Saturday was a 'pea-souper' when I ventured out of the caravan at Kinkell Braes to head down by the East Sands for my early morning walk. On the brae the St Andrews flag flew in the mist as battles of old. There is a popular photo point place at the top of brae before walking down. I myself have taken many a picture of the East Sands and harbour from there but not to be at this time because of the poor visibility. It was still soothing to hear the surge of the sea and gulls unearthing in me a childlike feeling. Down on level ground I passed by the many benches in memory of certain family members who like myself love St Andrews. The low cloud and mist around the harbour made an interesting picture at the birthplace of my gt grandmother.

I headed for The Pends and into Eastern Cemetery to pay my respect to her brother, sister and parents. It is warming for me to know that in recent years my wife and I have found final resting places of whom I descend from amongst the ruins of St Andrews. Many an hour over the years has been spent in search of names.

'In thought I cross the family divide' is a line in my poem Sojourn in St Andrews. It is about my guilty feeling over a decade ago when in St Andrews. Here was I, a Wulfrunian boy realising and accepting I had a past somewhere other than Wolverhampton. I had always thought that at sometime a Scottish relation may step forward.

'Will I shake another by hand' is another line from my poem. Well I did so, at the gate of the Cathedral Ruins on Sunday afternoon. His name is Paul Owen, a direct cousin who has been a Caddie on the Old Course for 20 years. Here is a surprise though, he's from Wolverhampton.

We were waiting to meet Paul as planned and I instantly
knew it was him from over 100 yards away as he walked
along the path in the ruins. It could have been a family
instinct because of his stride and profile.

It was an enjoyable and emotional afternoon and evening
with Paul and his partner Jacki as we got to know each
other. It was last summer that I was told by Joey, his brother
that he lived in St Andrews. Neither of us knew of each
others link to St Andrews and accordingly he has been
talking of me ever since. This meeting made the trip
worthwhile.

One more early walk down by the Saltire flag on Kinkell Braes which proved to be the best morning of our stay, typical as we were heading home.

The journey between Codsall and Fife kept on happening and over the years my wife and I have searched many graveyards in Scotland and looked at hundreds if not thousands of headstones. We were successful in finding some graves and when in St Andrews my early morning walk takes in an ancestral visit with a view of the East Sands. Visibility was poor the April 2014 morning when I made my early morning visit to the Eastern Cemetery. So poor that I could not see the caravan site where we were staying up on the Kinkle Braes from my gt. gt. Grandparents final resting place. Attracting my attention when walking the hill back to the site were a small cluster of bluebells.

Cannae see Kinkell Braes today
Mr Traill ©

2014

Murky is the April morning,
it didnae matter
my feet went childlike pitter-patter
towards the East Sands
this murky April morning

Making my way to the Harbour
through Mill Port Arch and up The Pends,
a slight incline, in St Andrews
where ancestral hurting mends

Cannae see Kinkle Braes today
Kinkle Braes cannae see
cannae see Kinkell Braes today Mr Traill.

Because of low lying cloud,
the surge of the sea is loud
cannae see Kinkell Braes today Mr Traill

Murky is the April morning
but still, my legs keep going

St Rule's Tower 'cause of clouds not showing
back along the path and up I scale
ahead of me is lunch and ale

Bluebells grow upon the crags o Kinkle Braes
even though the clouds do veil, Mr Traill
Bluebells grow upon the crags o Kinkle Braes

We were a right pair Lynne and myself on our next trip
having made and wrapped up sausage sandwiches and
searched for a flask to make some tea. Don't know if we are
holidaying on a budget or not but that was our breakfast a
couple of hours into our journey to Fife. Following that it
was a drive through heavy rain from the border to
Hamilton on the M74. This would be the first week in
August 2014 as we had decided to have a few days at short
notice.

It was a pleasant meeting we had with Fife poet Robert
Brews and his wife Sally. We were treated to lunch at Clio's
in Rosyth as we all got to know each other. Bob and myself
share a similar interest of writing.

After our goodbyes we made our way to our B&B in St
Michaels near Leuchars. We were not disappointed with the
Shangri-La and the excellent reviews that we had found
were true to their word

Late afternoon was the short drive to Tayport to get
accustomed to our much needed holiday. Broughty Ferry
looked fine at the other side of the Tay and the only sound
was birds feeding on the river surface. Within the hour we
were in our car in Broughty Ferry struggling to see Tayport
because of rain and poor visibility.

The Road That Takes Me Home ©

2014

The road to where I'm going
is the road from where we came,
the road that leads from home to home
is a road that takes my name

The road that calls me northward
was worth the fouling rain
and that road that starts by my front door
shall see me home again

Ay, that road shall drive me southward
back to the Midlands from where we came,
and that road that ends by my front door
shall see me home again

At a couple of minutes to 6.00am the north east coast train sped northwards over the railway bridge at St Michaels in Fife. It was a bright and brisk August 2014 morning and the decision to get my fleece from out of the car was a good idea. I was undecided what route to take on my walk then opted for a short there and back on the road to Cupar. With these being fast main roads for commuters to Dundee and Fife it was a strictly footpath only walk.

By an open broken old gate to a field by Carrick Cottage I noticed a lovely north view to the brae that I shall have to find if it has a name (Straiton Hill). Whilst gazing I watched a fox running through the long grass in the field.

The visibility this morning was excellent and with being

only a few miles to the Tay, in the distance I caught sight of Craigowl Hill the highest of the Sidlaws that overlooks Dundee.

This mind of mine was active as I imagined those Bennet's and Traill's of ours travelling these roads many, many years ago.

I walked back to the crossroads and on the B945 for a few hundred yards towards Tayport before turning back to the Shangri-la Guest House. Whilst tidying up this piece of writing in the garden, the horses are running and grazing in the field beyond.

Fife am I Early or Fifty Years Late? ©

2014

Fife you look grand this morning,
as your chill wind cuts through my clothes,
Fife you look grand this morning
now everyone reading this knows.

That wind I have mentioned that cuts through my skin
Fife I can feel you, you are deep down within,
I write these words by that broken old gate
Fife am I early or fifty years late?
Fife, ... you were well worth the wait.

We made our way to Cupar on a fine sunny morning after a
gorgeous Scottish breakfast at Shangri-la. I was approached
by a gentleman there after he noticed that I had taken a
photo of an unusual alley sign. TAK TENT O SMA THINGS
was the name and Malcolm Truesdale of Cupar Heritage
was the man who spoke to me. Malcolm could tell of my
interest and explained that there is many a wynd and
vennel around Cupar.

Ladybank, where my Dad came from, was next on our
visiting list. I parked up near to the war memorial as usual
and spent the next thirty minutes absorbing the village.

We paid our usual respects at Kingskettle and then headed
for Elie in the East Neuk. It was here that I stumbled upon
when walking the Coastal Path in 2007 and could not
believe how simple and lovely it is. We refreshed at the Ship
Inn where I once messaged back that I was having the best
pint in the best pub with the best view ever.

St Andrews was calling and after admiring the stunning
view from Kinkell Braes, we parked up at East Sands where
earlier this year I had my pre-60th photo taken. As an
addition this is a favoured and most walked path of mine in
Fife.

It was here in 2008 that I arrived at 6.00am after one of my overnight drives. I was walking the coastal path and wish that I had time to do some more. My point to point now stands from Delmeney near Edinburgh to Broughty Ferry. (Since writing I have reached Carnoustie).

We had heard of the 20 minute delays at Guardbridge because of resurfacing the bridge but that turned out to be a good thirty five which tested our patience very much so. We were heading to the Bell Rock Tavern in Tayport for our evening meal.

Afterwards we relaxed in the harbour and agreed that it is such a peaceful natural setting without the commercialisation. This is where our Bennet line first came over the Tay from Dundee to live about a hundred and ten years earlier. Strange but rewarding feeling to see the views what they would have been familiar with.

The evening sun was low as we pulled in to a public viewing point overlooking Dundee. It was still unbelievably quiet and the visibility was perfect as we watched the Sailing Club near Broughty Ferry doing what they do well. Nothing quite like the sight of sails on glistening water. Turning to look towards the Road Bridge and Dundee captured a fantastic evening scene.

Again at a couple of minutes to 6.00am I stepped out of the Shangri-la at St Michaels for an early morning stroll. People may consider this strange but early morning marathon training is well set within me albeit at a slower pace. Walking to Leuchers and back on the A914 was the plan.

I entered the St Michaels Golf Course to look on the railway bridge to be welcomed by a marvellous view. This is also the entrance to the cemetery but gates looked locked.

In 2008 when walking the coastal path, I can recall seeing the lovely St Athernase Church on the corner of the Pitlethie Road in Leuchars. Along there and within 25 yards little did I know that an Owen and cousin of mine from Wolverhampton resided.

On the return leg I once again stopped at the golf course to

admire what the morning has to offer. It was like walking
out onto a stage and the countryside was an audience.

The Bridge That I Cross o'er
in St Michaels ©

2014

One lang mile to Leuchers
one mile at most,
one morning out there
if big headed I would boast

I felt praised and devoted
more fortunate I noted,
now let me imagine being a star
even though I'm that by far

The bridge that I cross o'er in St Michaels
something I find to please my mind,
ay, a fantastic view, arriving was I
before the Golfers do

That bridge that I cross o'er in St Michaels
there I was being adored,
people there waiting
and my audience applaud

The bridge that I cross o'er in St Michaels
raised and brought me back to earth,
I could not act or sing a word
I was speechless, for what it is worth

It was a huge decision this morning to get up early and drive away from the Shangri-la at 5.05am. Ten minutes later I was crossing the Tay Bridge on route for Broughty Castle where I parked the car. It was time to get some Wulfrunian footprints in Angus. My plan was to walk northward eastward to Carnoustie over 6 miles along the coast. This was to add to my 2007 and 2008 of the Fife Coastal Path into Dundee. Since then I have added a stretch from Seagate Bus Station to Broughty Castle. Now it was another piece of Scottish coast that I can add to my journey.

Within minutes I was walking past a football pitch on the outskirts of Broughty. Being the birthplace of Frank Munro I imagined him playing there as boy and the crisp wind blowing in from the Tay.

I soon passed through Monifieth and got then confused around the Barry Burden Army base which set me back a while. I got back on track walking along the cycle path and arrived at Carnoustie Golf Course at Barry Links Station. My ancestral walk was completed for now and at 7.45am I was waiting at a bus stop to take me back to Broughty Ferry. I was soon driving back to the Shangri-la for breakfast and to plan for the day ahead.

"Even though it's nae the coast o' Fife
this is now Angus, and it's my life"

Later that day we had arranged to meet our new friends from the Shangri-la in Tickety Boo's after the Dundee v Kilmarnock game. They gave us directions although I had a good idea where the bar was. Whilst waiting outside at a pavement table, my imaginative mind was active as I have found ancestry addresses in this area of Dundee. I took a couple of photos, wrote a poem and then early this morning found a picture on Lost Dundee's Facebook page that could be the scene I had in mind.

At Tickety Boo's in Dundee ©

2014

On the corner of Seagate
there's a bar on Commercial Street,
Tickety Boo's in Dundee
on a Saturday eve we did meet
And my mind was engaged therein
days of the nineteen century,
down the street of Seagate,
there trod ancestors feet
Outside of Tickety Boo's
in captivating company of today,
then Bennet's, Traill's and Anderson's,

311

Smith's, Reid's, Brown's they passed this way
See those wearing Victorian clothes
by St Paul's the women waved,
men's hats were raised with a welcome home
pleasant pictures are dearly saved
Then Edwardian Dundonians
they shout and call my name,
I raise my glass as they walk passed
from those this descendant came
Only imagination
and realistic I may add too,
outside the claret frontage
of Dundee's Tickety Boo's
Hear the Jute Weavers laughing
emphatically the Dockers were singing,
it all seemed practically true
there at Tickety Boo's

She Came a' Courting With Me ©

2014

She must love me
because she wanted to
come a' courting with me in Parkfields,
and she wanted to marry me
when, we were too young,
occasionally we dance to
an old song, we used to dance to.

She must love me
because she wanted to
have children with me,

when we were young,
we built a home in Parkfields
when we were young

Don't get me wrong,
we argued and we fought,
but together we brought,
a future for our collective family
going forward, we moved to Codsall

She has always been the clever one,
the clever one of our partnership,
'cause I'm useless at finances,
but even now, she wants to hold me
when we are at functions and dances

She must love me
because she wanted to
come to Scotland with me,
would she marry me again?
Dare I ask,
would she marry me?
what a difficult task

What a difficult question
when life takes us in another direction,

314

into life of being grandparents
and she's brilliant at doing all that,
she changes plans at the drop of a hat

She must love me
because she wanted to
come a' courting with me,
back in Parkfields

Would she come a' courting again?
Dare I ask,
would she come a' courting?
What a difficult task

Occasionally we dance to,
an old song we used to dance to,
I think I'm in with a chance!

In August of 2013, whilst on the road home towards the Forth Road Bridge, I admitted to my wife that "it actually hurts to be leaving Fife", but why?

It must be all that I have found about Fife in recent years, people and places, and I'm probably only scratching the surface.

'I took one more picture for Hector', I was once told that the Lomond Hills was a favoured view before becoming one of mine. Even to the point of having a painting of them by Leslie Broadfield, a relative in Wolverhampton.

It has been 60 years and more since 'our Fifer' departed to join the British Army, 'his bloodline runs on in England', as I wrote in my poem The Kingdom of Fife, back in 2002.

Our Bonnie Four, Aaron, Liam, Kiera-Marie and Caitlyn, our Fifers four, and he has more!

Fife by this time has a homely feel and the drive always lifts my spirit. Two hours into the journey and the Lake District views are lovely. After a break the signs to Carlisle and then Scotland appear and it is noticeable that the temperature gauge in the car drops. It has been spoken about between Lynne and myself as to how long I could do the drive. The years have fled by since first travelling to Fife and it would be difficult now to live without having a few visits throughout the year,

Lanarkshire looked mysteriously lovely with low lying mist and part visible wind turbines. Within a few minutes we drove into a view of colourful scenery as the morning sun started burning away the cloud. It had just turned 9.00am on this late September Monday morning of 2014 and almost 4 hours into our journey to Fife. An hour later we were parked up just outside Dalgety Bay overlooking the Forth and spectacular views. Memories of first walking the coastal path in 2007 came flooding back.

Food shopping in Kirkcaldy was the next job on our list and then to Leven where we relaxed and had lunch by the sands. Once again it was reminiscing as it was here on this beach that I stepped out on in 2008 for my second stage of my walk. It was a dawn start and I recall the dark sky and coastline. I wrote 'The Silver Trail to Crail' afterwards. What was missing from that morning were the two chimneys of Methil Power Station that were demolished in June 2011. They were industrially unique and featured in two of artist Jack Vettriano's paintings.

Our private caravan booking on the Kinkell Braes proved to be a good choice with a huge balcony and fabulous view. Included in that view was the East Sands and Shorehead, birthplace of my gt grandmother (Oh Isabella). Later that afternoon a social meeting with a Wolverhampton Owen cousin of mine at the Dunvegan Hotel "the perfect 19th hole" as per one famous golfer.

At 7.50am next morning I am having a wee browse about the Old Course where they are setting up for the Alfred Dunhill Links Championship. The promotional Mercedes vehicles are quite evident about St Andrews. Earlier I was to be in conversation with a student who was training hard by running up and down the steep path from the harbour to the castle. "I was once a marathon runner", I told him, so I understood as to why he found it challenging.

Upon my return walk I called by the war memorial and cleared cobwebs from the name of Thomas Loch Traill. At Easter Cemetery and not like the last time, I could see Kinkell Braes today Mr Traill, through the haze of the bright morning that it has turned out to be.

Red Sunrise at St Andrews ©

2014

I wanted to see the first light in St Andrews,
to be where the red sun there shall rise,
I wanted to see the first light in St Andrews,
and there I watched, the first light with my eyes,
the red sunrise in St Andrews.

Listening to waves
listening to, a three second surge,
and then the red sun did emerge,
out in the coastline,
the dark coastline at St Andrews,

How the grey sky mixed,
with the North Sea at St Andrews,
then came the red sunrise
the red sunrise intervened,
here in St Andrews

I wanted to see the first light in St Andrews,
to be where the red sun there shall rise,
I wanted to see the first light in St Andrews,

There I saw, the first light in St Andrews,
there I saw the red sunrise,
with my own eyes,
the red sunrise in St Andrews.

After a late breakfast and shower it was a stroll down the same route towards the harbour and a couple of hours in St Andrews. The morning was unbelievingly warm. Early afternoon we headed for the Old Course and although not golfers we took in the atmosphere and build-up of the above mentioned championship. We then relaxed on the West Sands that was made famous in 1981 for filming the beach scene in Chariots of Fire. The sea was calm and a deeper blue than the light sky with no mixing of colours this time.

Within minutes the peace was shattered for a short time as around forty schoolchildren came running on to the beach. They were either re-enacting the Chariots of Fire or heading for the sea. I watched as a lad took his shoes and socks off and went waist deep into the water. His schoolteacher was soon to be there and appeared to have a word. 'There's always one' was the thought.

Whilst relaxing we had been watching some kind of radio controlled aeroplane flying about over the beach and then all of a sudden it was hovering about us. I could only think that it was a camera in practice for the Dunhill Golf Championship so we were on our best behaviour in case we were being filmed.

Another social meeting with more of the Owen family from Wolverhampton at the Dunvegan Hotel. Who would have thought that this would ever happen? It was a monumental moment for the family which pleased my mother very much so as she is the last surviving of those Owen children.

We headed back along North Street and along the coast to our caravan on the Kinkell Braes on this early calm evening. We watched as a flock of gulls were active out in the sea as they must have discovered a shoal of fish to feed on. Our evening dinner of chicken and vegetables was a joy to prepare and eat. At around 8pm we heard the first rain of our break falling on the caravan roof.

I looked down at my shoes and trousers to see that they were soaked up to my knees. I was almost at the summit of West Lomond (522m / 1713ft) and not yet had my breakfast. It was pitch-black when I departed the caravan site and had decided to park near Gateside, further west in Fife. The plan was to reach the summit as near to dawn as possible. Things did not go as I expected as I found it difficult to find a suitable place to park and start walking. A false start and then a rethink to return to Bonnet Stane parking area and made my ascend from there.

On route I had driven through Strathmiglo which was once the main road before the A91 by-pass in the 1970's. When looking at the dwellings it is easy to imagine the bygone days with the distinctive town house steeple and children playing in the street and only a horse and cart to beware of. This early morning is a picture of the modern age with countless parked vehicles.

In 2009 when calling into the Strath pub I was to engage in conversation with a lady behind the bar. She was involved with the local football team Strathmiglo United. This was to lead into a complimentary message in my guest book on my website;

Just had the time to look at your fabulous site. Really great stories and poetry, Fife tourism should be featuring your work!. Thanks for your mention of Strathmiglo United and please visit us when you are in the area. Best wishes, John and Sheila. (Comment by:John Schofield)

In 2014 came the news that John and Sheila were to stand down from their duties after being a massive part of the football club to start a new life in Dunfermline. I forwarded my best wishes to the Facebook page. According to their website Association Football has been played in Strathmiglo for over 100 years.

Most people I know have been met through the game of
football. It is a world wide link. It lives and breathes inside
of us, it spoils our week if out team loses and lifts us when
we win. A none football fan does not understand. They don't
have one ear to the radio on a Saturday afternoon. Bill
Shankly once said, "It's more important than life or death".
We all know it was a tongue in cheek remark but we
understand what he meant.

The Strath Won the Fife Cup ©

2009

Perhaps one day I shall travel
Through the Lake District and the borderland.
Perhaps one day I shall be 'neath a Lomond Hill
Perhaps one day I shall travel, perhaps I will.

Perhaps one day I shall travel
Through Cowdenbeath and Glenrothes,
Perhaps one day I shall go to Strathmiglo.

Perhaps one day I shall be close-up
To the pitch o' the Strath who won the Fife Cup,
Perhaps one day I shall see their field of green,
Perhaps one day thinks this man,
This auld has been.

Now remember, Strathmiglo are a founder member,
Of the Kingdom Caledonian AFA,
Perhaps that day I'll find the answer before I pack-up
Can you sup from the Fife Cup?

Perhaps one day I shall travel
Glasgow, an hour or so from Strathmiglo,
Living fitba life, breathing football breath,
"More serious" said Shank's "than life or death."

Whenever near Strathmiglo I think of a fellow that I know
named John Paton. He lives in my village of Codsall,
Staffordshire and has ancestry lineage to Strathmiglo. He
has an interesting family tree that traces back there to the
18th century. John descends from another John Paton, born
in Strathmiglo in 1746 who married Janet Wilson in 1776.
His line then leads to Cumberland, to Barony in Lanarkshire
and to Aston, Birmingham. John, son of Charles W. Paton
was born in 1939 and moved to Wolverhampton in 1983
where he was a publican until retiring to Codsall in 1992.

Returning back to my climb of West Lomond, which I felt I had to do soon as the clock of father-time was ticking fast. It turned out to be the most difficult challenge of my later life as it was a series of heights that appeared never ending. There were many pauses to rest and catch my breath and the visibility was poor. Nearing the summit the mist and cloud dropped and I couldn't see a thing. I was starting to get concerned and pleased that I had put my sat-nav in my bag just in case. I watched as the cloud wrapped around the Lomonds and made my descent.

My ageing knees were tested beyond anything I had ever experienced as the wind picked-up strength. Within a second it stopped and became as calm as you could imagine allowing me to collect my thoughts. I paused and looked

down on the Howe of Fife and damned Scotland for making
me want to do this. Robert Brews, a Fife writer and poet,
was to later send me this message "your Wulfrunian
footsteps will be forever in the high hills, Robbie"

The journey back to St Andrews was past the road signs to
Collessie, dad's birthplace and Ladybank his childhood
home. Lynne cussed me when I got back for doing this
challenge and told me I had a blood-shot eye. I blamed it on
Hector Bennet, my gt grandfather for loving the view of the
Lomonds.

I look into the lines of my poem *The Kingdom of Fife* as a
different man from when it was written in 2002. I have
wandered and roamed many of those lanes with walls of
stone. I have been to the cottage where dad was born. There
is not any smoke from the railway these days but I have
stood on Ladybank Station. If he wanted to climb the
Lomonds and never did, then I have done so in his place. I
have been north to the Firth of Tay and to the churches of
Collessie and Cupar. I am also very often in St Andrews Bay.
I have ended and started a coastal walk at Crail. It's a fact
that this Scotsman's bloodline runs on now in England and
Bennet Kennedy roots, and more lie in Fife. We do honour
the land that we live in, and definitely for me, the Kingdom
is a part of my life.

Guid Mornin' Isabella ©

2014

I walk along my favoured path
in a special place,
the breeze is a wee bit chilling
upon the brae there in my face

Guid mornin' Isabella
I think of you without fail,
guid mornin' Isabella
and to you, my James Traill,
my Elizabeth Brown,
wish that you could see me now
on the Kinkell Braes, heading on down

Loud is the surge
louder than the last time,
loud is the surge by the sands,
feeling safe in your hands

I walk along my favoured path
in my special place,
the breeze is a wee less chilling
by the sands there in my face

Louder is the surge
louder is the surge by the sands,
ay, louder, louder is the surge,
stronger is the feeling by the sands
ay, stronger, stronger is the felling,
of being safe in your hands

Safe in your hands
Guid mornin' Isabella

There was plenty activity this bright and sunny October morning by the Old Course. Today was the first day of the Dunhill Golf Championship and everything looked like all had to be in order. I was on the lookout for a cousin of mine, from Wolverhampton who is a caddie here for a well known ex-professional footballer who I believe is playing today. Whilst writing this I noticed the Irish Rugby player Brian O'Driscoll warming-up.

I had made my way down from the Kinkell Braes and into Market Street calling into the Eastern Cemetery along the way. I always feel a presence of family in St Andrews and a belonging here. It is no wonder that there was a calling inside of me when here on work related business 12 years earlier. Since then I have found an enormous amount of our Scottish ancestry and there is far more that I will never unearth. My return was along the coastal path passing Martyrs Monument and Castle ruins and up the Kinkell Braes, that chilling wind was now refreshing.

The fishermen looked busy tending nets and loading their catch in Pittenweem this mid-day. We were on our way to the Upper Largo Hotel to have lunch with Fife Poet Robert

Brews and his wife Sally. Bob and I have a common interest of writing and he is very busy with the launch of his second book.

The weather forecast was all change after today with high winds and lower temperature. Next morning the weather girl announced that more rain was to fall on Friday than in all of September. Before then it was a walk down the brae and into St Andrews for our last evening. We laughed as a group of students ran into the sea for a chilling dip. They were soon out though and ran back to their small beach fire that they had burning.

The evening sun shining on the east coast from the west gives a different picture than I usually take. From the height of the cliff path by the cannons we looked out to see white clouds with shades of pale red. A couple of hours later was the return walk but this time in the dark eating chips from a cardboard box. "You sure know how to treat a girl", said Lynne as we listened to the sea and struggled to see the path that we were walking on.

Overnight we were awakened by the blustering wind that I found were 40 to 50 mph that always seems worse in a caravan. It is early Friday morning and I listen intently to the local traffic news for the Forth Road Bridge.

Although it was not inviting weather I still had a brisk walk along my favoured path. The East Sands was almost deserted except for a solitary dog walker. You could tell that there was a brightening effort of a light sky but was being beaten by the enormity of dark grey clouds. My final respects at Eastern Cemetery then back along the path and up the 150 ageing strides to Kinkell Braes.

Farewell Isabella ©

2014

Farewell Isabella
I think of you without fail,
farewell Isabella
and to you, my James Traill,
my Elizabeth Brown,
wish that you could see me now
climbing up the Kinkell Braes,
then heading on down,
heading on down to England

It was forecast a rainy drive home to Codsall but before doing so we had a couple of calls to make. One was to Monkstown, Ladybank to take a photo from there of the Lomonds. This would have been the Bennet's view of the hills and I wish that they would have known that one of their own was to climb them. The other was to Kingskettle Cemetery where I looked up again at the Lomonds to see that they were clouding over. Although 6 years in between, I had the satisfaction that I have climbed both "Paps of Fife" as they are known locally. It was time to get on the road to Codsall from home to home. The usual feelings of deserting and returning were surfacing.

Later that evening in our kitchen at home I turned over the page of the calendar from September to October, two days in both months needed marking off. I done so with emotions of sadness and contentment created by another few days in Fife.

Hurting of Leaving Fife ©

2013

Bright and early, we took the road to Fife
a well earned few days, that was our plan
up in ancient St Andrews,
a long time togetherness of woman and man

We took the road to Kirkcaldy
shopped and walked the prom,
my brain was thinking of kin
who's here or have my Kennedy's gone?

Surely though my kin have seen
surely my Kennedy's have seen Edinburgh gleam?
in light like this afternoon
from Kirkcaldy, the lang toun, we hit the road soon

On the road to St Andrews

'St Andreas' my Traill's by the Northern Sea,
architectural ruins, Old Tom Morris, golfing history,
fashionable and vibrant is the air, thanks to the university

I have a pleasing, pleasing feeling
this laddies head is reeling,
Fife, you're looking grand
beat does my heart in a pipe and drum band

We took the road to Collessie
Collessie she captured me again,
weather forecast was awful,
but the threat of rain never came

I took one more picture for Hector
one more picture of the Lomond Hills,
watched the Lomonds lighten as they do,
I took one more picture, then found I'd took two!

Soon we were homeward bound
to our bonnie Grandchildren, little un's sound
the years they fly too fast
taking the road to the future and past

I have a guilty, guilty feeling

like a laddie caught stealing
Fife, am I deserting?
Going home, leaving Fife and it's hurting.

Aye it hurts, and this auld laddie's blurting
stand up man, 'tuck yer shirt in'
'you've bonnie four and a home in two places'
Aye, Bonnie four, Bonnie four little faces.

Not so early, we took the road from Fife
a well earned few days cause of a Fifer we had
up with the Traill's in ancient St Andrews
a long time togetherness, now a Nan and Grandad.

A lang time togetherness, ye Lassie's an' Lad.

Aye, Bonnie four an' could th' future bring more?

337

It takes approximately 3 hours to cross over the Scottish border from my home in Codsall. It is then almost another 2 hours to reach the Forth Road Bridge. I experience a feeling of excitement when I am in the vicinity of the bridges. I can only describe it to be childlike as when the curtains are drawn open at a picture show or a pantomime. Whatever, it's magnificent enough for me to describe it as a symbolic scene. On another note, there's a hurt and a calling inside for me to come back, after all, I have good reason to.

Saying Goodbye to Fife ©

2007

Saying goodbye to Fife
Is uncanny it really is,
I perceive the sign a side of the road
As I approach the Forth Road Bridge.
Another wee visit has now gone by
To satisfy my longing,
Saying goodbye to Fife
Where I have a strong bond of belonging.
Come speed the day that I return
Come speed the hour that I shall see,
The symbolic scene preceding the kingdom
Fife will smile and welcome me.

Dads' family had passed-on and moved around this British land and beyond. Who knows who our kin are in Scotland. In 2011 someone in the USA sent me an interesting e-mail. She also descends from Hector Bennet of Dundee.

"I happened upon your site while doing family research. I greatly enjoyed not only your poems, but also your thoughtful narrative and pictures. Incidentally, my Great Great Grandmother was Jessie Smith Bennet, the sister of your Hector, who left Scotland in 1925."

Awa' wi' th' Penguins in Dundee

On Saturday 20th June 2009 I was in the process of penning this rhyme about Wolverhampton. All the miles that I travel I always look for Wolverhampton on road and motorway signs. Approaching I always look for the church of St Peters. I needed a picture to go with the poem and remembered when I lived that side of town occasionally I would go to the top of Sedgley Beacon for the panoramic view. You can see Birmingham, Worcestershire, and the Wrekin in Shropshire and of course St Peters Church Wolverhampton.

I made my way to the height of Sedgley Beacon for the first time in over 20 years and found it to be a lovely clear day.

Inherent Wolverhampton ©

2009

Wherever the leather on my shoes take me to
A far off beach, a stretch of coast a fabulous view
I always head back home
Home to Wolverhampton
Where my family reside
Where they all abide
The surroundings of Wolverhampton

Conscious of the day and come the time
I've read the script and I see the homebound sign
Be not my blood thick and thorough,
… I'm bounty of the borough of Wolverhampton

Dear old Dudley Street, Grand Theatre and Queens Square
St Peters, prominently standing there
St Peters, can't recall ever being inside
Wolverhampton, where my family reside

Childhood excitement of shop windows in Wolverhampton
Easily produced what my dear mother introduced
She loves Wolverhampton
Where memories were made, I miss the Arcade
Up town in Wolverhampton

…Those memories won't fade,
My mother and I in the glistening Arcade
Inherent Wolverhampton

Friends and family sought and caught a bus,
Each and every one of us
To and fro Stafford Street or Pipers Row
The buses would go
To the estates of Wolverhampton

Wolverhampton
I speak your tongue,
Your children I grew up among
Boy's pumps to a size seven shoe
Wolverhampton, what more can I offer you?

High on Sedgley Beacon today like an eagle I perch
Looking for St Peters church
St Peters, Wolverhampton
St Peters, can't recall ever being inside
Wolverhampton, where my family reside

Wherever the leather on my shoes take me to
Tyres wear and tear with the miles that I do
Driving a stack and heading back to Wolverhampton
Where my family reside

344

Where they all abide
The surroundings of Wolverhampton

Dear old Dudley Street, Grand Theatre and Queens Square
Home in Wolverhampton
I'm going home to my family back there

Although not a poem about Fife, this is about my wife and I by the Solway Firth that divides England and Scotland. Other than actually walking the Fife Coastal Path, she has been with me since we were teenagers and in many a mile of my journey. This was 2008 on a festive break in Dumfries. It could be said that she has been a long suffering lassie.

May Th' Lovely Lassie ©

2008

She walked on ice on th' Solway Firth
I do remember
She walked on ice on th' Solway Firth
Late on last December
May th' lovely lassie
Always love this laddie o'

She walked with me at Sandyhills
Fields were a' white o' frost
She walked with me at Sandyhills
O'er frozen dunes we crossed
May th' lovely lassie
Always with this laddie go

She walked with me in gallivant youth
Down th' rocky road an' kyle
She walked with me in gallivant youth
We ventured down th' aisle
She walked to me my bride in white
Oh, my heart did swoon
She walked to me my bride in white
One day in June

She walked on ice on th' Solway Firth
O'er thirty years thereafter
She walked on ice on th' Solway Firth
Lambent love an' laughter
May th' lovely lassie
Always love this laddie o'
May th' lovely lassie
Always with this laddie go

She walked on ice on th' Solway Firth

May th' lovely lassie
Always love this laddie o'

The journey hopefully will go on by wife and myself,
children or grandchildren and the words for new writing of
Fife keep coming.

Our bonnie grandchildren, Aaron, the eldest born on the
day when Robert the Bruce became King.

Next came Liam, his cousin, who teaches me about
Dinosaurs and the natural world.

Then his sister, Kiera-Marie, a pretty dark haired Princess,
who shares a birthday with my dad.

Then her blonde haired cousin Caitlyn, with striking blue
eyes, born on the first of May where traditionally in St
Andrews students run into the sea at dawn.

Last but not least, for those born after my words went to
print, a poem written in 2007, Do I Know You?

Do I Know You? ©

2007

Do I know you?

You reading my words,

Do I know you?

Do my words interest you?

Do they?

Is there anything that you want to tell me?

Is there?

Is there anything you want to ask?

If you've got this far you are intrigued,

you may have loved me,

Even though you may or may not even know me.

It's now 2007,

Where are you?

If you are my flesh and blood then I love you,

I really do.

My wish is that I inspire you,

Even if I did, or I didn't know you.

So let me return to the question, do I know you?

I feel that I do.

Upon discussing a recent snippet of a mention of my writing on a Scottish radio station, "you've certainly left your footprints in Fife Robbie" said my mother.

"In your lifetime dad, you didn't know,
that there would be a calling,
back to your birth land, there I would go,
feelings for Fife, mysteriously flirts,
not known in your lifetime dad,
and I admit that it hurts"

"Lang may yer lum reek"

Wulfrunian Footprints in Fife, Copyright ©

Robbie Kennedy Bennett 2014

Printed in Great Britain
by Amazon.co.uk, Ltd.,
Marston Gate.